Exam Grade Booster

GCSE German

Dan Grimwood & Liam Porritt

Checked and approved by:

Lindsay McDonald	Head of Modern Languages, Tonbridge School MA in Modern Languages (French & German), St Edmund Hall, University of Oxford
Sholto Kerr	Head of German, Tonbridge School BA in German, University of Birmingham
Lionel Austin	Examiner for numerous exam boards Previous Head of Modern Languages, Tonbridge School & German teacher for over 30 years
Henrik Sachs	Native German speaker with fluent English Student at the University of Cambridge
Graham Samuels	Teacher of French and German, Woodbridge High School, Redbridge BA in French and German, Royal Holloway University MEd Educational Research, University of Cambridge

Published by Exam Grade Booster
(Publisher prefix 978-0-9930429)
www.examgradebooster.co.uk

ISBN-13:   *978-0-9930429-2-8*

Disclaimer

The authors and named checkers and approvers of this publication give no guarantee of improved examination performance nor will they be held responsible for any mistakes which may appear in this publication. They are not responsible if this publication, in any way, has a detrimental effect on its reader(s) or any other persons. This publication offers suggestions which have produced results for the authors, but does not in any way state that these methods are the only ways of succeeding in GCSE or IGCSE examinations. All of the information given may not be entirely correct for all examination boards. The information given will not be inclusive of everything required for every examination board.

Credit

Special thanks go to Graham Samuels who must be credited with showing us the acronym *'CROATIANS'*, as used on pg. 49.

OTHER BOOKS BY LIAM PORRITT

Exam Grade Booster: GCSE French

Exam Grade Booster: GCSE Spanish

Exam Grade Booster: IGCSE Chemistry Edexcel

The Rules of Revision

OTHER BOOKS IN THIS SERIES

Exam Grade Booster: GCSE English

Exam Grade Booster: IGCSE Biology Edexcel

Exam Grade Booster: IGCSE Physics Edexcel

Contents

About Us

Dan Grimwood

I will always be grateful for the opportunities which became available to me at school, and for those which have arisen following academic success there. In Exam Grade Booster I saw a chance to share with other students some of what Liam and I have had access to.

For as long as I have been studying it, German has been a favourite of mine. That should become clear as you read the following pages! However, despite its importance as a key to a rich and diverse culture, and its desirability in the business world, let alone the fact of its 100 million native speakers, the number of students studying German in the UK is dwindling. This book, then, has been written to help you seize the opportunity of being part of a select group in an advantageous and gratifying position. Use it well and work hard.

Liam Porritt

I have been extremely fortunate to attend one of the best schools in the country and in this book Dan and I aim to share the outstanding, exam-focused teaching which has led to our success. I believe our experience and knowledge of revising for and then taking GCSE and IGCSE examinations make this guide uniquely suited to preparing any student for success in their own German exams.

I am also the author of *Exam Grade Booster: GCSE French* and *Exam Grade Booster: GCSE Spanish*, with the former highly reviewed by The Independent Schools' Modern Languages Association. I firmly believe that this guide will enable any student, willing to spend a little time and effort, to boost their grade and make the most of their potential. My goal is to share the techniques and tricks I have learnt while studying languages, particularly those which others can emulate in both the revision process and the exam room itself.

How to Use this Book

This book is designed to boost your German GCSE or IGCSE grade. It is suitable for both UK and International qualifications for all examination boards.

The book has three sections:

- The first section is designed to outline exactly what is required in each of the four parts of your German examination (writing, oral, reading and listening) in order for you to achieve better results.
- The second section will then target the areas of your German exam which you can improve using our tried and tested methods. It is essentially a toolbox of things you need to boost your grade.
- The final part will give you specific essential learning to do. It contains the information you absolutely must know as well as clever hints and tips to help you understand the tricky bits.

The first section should be read through as you would read any ordinary book from start to finish. The second and third sections do not have any particular order, so we advise you to flick through and pick out the areas you feel will be most useful.

There are some sections which are only applicable for either GCSE or IGCSE students, so skip over any bits which are not relevant to you. They are clearly marked.

Note: Throughout the book, you will see the names of the tenses that exist in German: Perfect, Simple Past (Preterite), Present, Future, etc. These refer to the normal type (or indicative mood) of the verb. However, the subjunctive mood is used a lot in German, often to express a conditional (e.g. *I would go, if I could*). Even if this is new to you, chances are, you already use the subjunctive without really knowing it! Have a look at the verbs section, which starts of pg. 85, for more information.

Section I

The Exam & What You Need To Do

Writing Examination

The writing examination is the **essay** component of the exam and will be marked according to the following three criteria:

1. **Communication**
2. **Use of language**
3. **Accuracy**

Communication

- Have you understood the assignment, and written appropriately (about the correct topic)?
- Do you respond to **all** the points of the assignment in your essay?
- Have you given opinions?
- Do you give justified reasons for the opinions expressed? E.g. why do you like or dislike something?
- Does your essay make sense?

If yes: you answer all the points clearly with reasons for why; and yes: the examiner can understand your essay, you will get **full marks** for this area.

So, how do you respond to all points of the assignment clearly?

Simple! All you have to do is write one paragraph for each point of the question. (We will explain more on this in a minute!)

The first and most crucial point about writing any essay in German is to make sure you write what you know, and don't write what you don't know. Do not be afraid to make up the content of your essay! The story of your essay does not have to be factually correct. The examiner does not know you and does not care if you have really done what you claim to have done. The exam is a test of your knowledge of the German language, not a test of how eventful your life has been. For example, if you went on holiday to Cambodia and ate fried tarantulas and played a xylophone made of bamboo, don't try to say all that because you don't know how to... And neither are you expected to! You can make up **anything** as long as it answers all the points of the essay.

So how do you answer all the points of the essay?

Standard GCSE (not IGCSE)

Depending on your task, you will be given two, three or four points to answer in your writing assignment(s), and these will test:

- Your use of tenses: the past, present and future
- Your vocabulary

For example, if your assignment were as follows:

You went to visit a friend in Germany last year and you are writing an article about your stay. Don't forget to include what you liked and what you disliked about your visit. Also include how it was different from what you normally do on holiday.

The article should also include recommendations of what other people should do when they visit a friend in Germany, with reasons for these recommendations.

In the above assignment, you can use the following tenses:

Tenses	To...
Perfect and Simple Past	Describe what you liked and disliked about your stay
Present	Say what you normally do and how this particular holiday was different from that
Future and Subjunctive II	Recommend things for people to do when they visit a friend in Germany

(If any of these tenses are not familiar to you, or you simply want to understand more about them, turn to the verbs section starting on pg. 85. There is a detailed explanation of the subjunctive on pg. 93.) So, a minute ago we said that we would explain more on having one paragraph for each point of the question, and here it is: for the above assignment, to gain full marks for **Communication**, simply write three paragraphs of roughly equal length. The first should be about what you liked and disliked about your stay, the second about what you normally do on holiday compared with what you did with your German friend, and the third should contain recommendations of what to do when visiting a friend in Germany. That's it.

IGCSE Only

You will be given four or five bullet points (in German) to respond to for each essay title and each of these will give you an opportunity to demonstrate your use of the various tenses and knowledge of vocabulary. For example, if the question were:

Sie haben einen Monat lang in den Ferien gearbeitet, um Geld zu verdienen. Schreiben Sie einen Artikel für eine Lokalzeitung, in dem es um Ihre Erfahrung geht, und zwar mit folgenden Informationen:

- *wo Sie gearbeitet haben*
- *was Sie machen mussten*
- *wie viel Geld Sie verdient haben, und wofür Sie normalerweise Ihr Geld ausgeben*
- *ob die Arbeitsstelle Ihnen gefallen hat*
- *Ihre Arbeitspläne diesen Sommer, und warum Sie das machen wollen*

Here, you could use the following tenses:

Tenses	To...
Perfect and Simple Past	Describe where you worked, what you had to do and how much money you earned
Present	Say what you normally spend your money on and your opinion of the work
Future and Subjunctive II	Describe what you will do this summer for work and why you would like to do this

(If any of these tenses are not familiar to you, or you simply want to understand more about them, turn to the verbs section starting on pg. 85. There is a detailed explanation of the subjunctive on pg. 93.) So, a minute ago we said that we would explain more on having one paragraph for each point of the question, and here it is: for the above question, to gain full marks for **Communication**, simply write five paragraphs of roughly equal length with each one answering one bullet point. The first paragraph should be about where you worked, the second about what the job involved you doing, and so on...That's it.

All Candidates

So, now you understand exactly how to structure your essay, you must understand the necessity for giving:

- Reasons why you did things
- Opinions of what you did
- Reasons for those opinions

If you want to get a high grade, this is not just important - it is **critical!** On every mark-scheme for every exam board there will be marks available for giving these three things, so make sure you give them all regularly throughout your essay. The German words *weil* and *da* meaning *because* or *since* should appear at regular intervals throughout your essay... If they don't, it means you are not justifying your actions or opinions enough.

Use of language

This mark is awarded according to how well you use German. Do you know the basic and more complex tenses? Do you use fluid constructions, with justified opinions throughout your essay? Do you use long sentences with connecting words (such as *therefore*) to link ideas? (Don't worry; we'll come onto all this later.)

FIRSTLY, IT IS ESSENTIAL YOU USE A VARIETY OF TENSES THROUGHOUT YOUR ESSAY TO BOOST YOUR GRADE.

You should know the basic tenses (present, perfect and future, as well as the simple past for the most important verbs) and if you don't, learn them ASAP (they are in the *Specific Essential Learning* section from pg. 90-99). We know it's dull, but they are crucial. However, using set phrases, it is easy to spice up these tenses and you should already know some pretty simple but effective vocabulary which can be manipulated to form a good essay.

To boost your mark in this area, all you have to do is use your knowledge of tenses combined with set phrases. Use both 'standard' phrases and 'opinion' phrases in the correct places and use them to form long sentences which make sense - easy! (There is a list of both these types of phrase starting on pg. 37.) It is vital that you use both of these types of phrase, as without opinion phrases you will not achieve a top grade - simple! Justifying why you do things throughout your essay is fundamental: always remember the three bullet points at the top of the previous page.

There is one more trick that will help to boost your **Use of language** mark: talking about other people. Throughout your essay you will spend most of the time talking about yourself, but to make it more interesting and to show off your grammar knowledge, try occasionally (maybe only twice) to mention someone else. For example: *Ich möchte bei einer Firma arbeiten, aber meine Freundin hat vor, an der Universität zu studieren.*

Accuracy

This is simply how few mistakes you make.

This is the hardest aspect to improve, and relies on your spelling, the correct use of tenses and agreement. This will be covered as fully as possible in the *Specific Essential Learning* section and also on pg. 61, which takes you through how to check your essays for grammar errors. However, if you learn the set phrases, and use them correctly, you can guarantee that they will be 100% correct, in both their use of vocabulary and tenses. Therefore, these phrases will improve your mark for both **Use of language** and **Accuracy**. We shall come onto **Accuracy** in more depth later, but in general:

GOLDEN RULE :
WRITE WHAT YOU KNOW, DON'T WRITE WHAT YOU DON'T KNOW
Don't think of a sentence in English and then try to translate that into German because you will make mistakes. Instead, think of what you know (phrases and vocab) and fit that into your essay.

We also have two other Golden Rules for your writing exam:

> **GOLDEN RULE :**
> **DON'T WRITE TOO MUCH**
> When you are given a word limit, don't go over it by too much because this will only increase the number of mistakes you make, and you will gain NO CREDIT for writing more.

> **GOLDEN RULE :**
> **USE PHRASES BUT DON'T FORCE THEM**
> When writing an essay, include as many phrases as you can, within reason. However, do not force them into an essay if they do not make sense. This will lower your **Communication** mark as well as your **Use of language** mark.

There is more specific advice on your writing exam, including a list of brilliant phrases to boost your mark for **Use of language** and advice which will definitely improve your **Accuracy**, starting on pg. 36.

However, we recommend you keep reading this section to find out how to boost your marks in your oral, reading and listening examinations, before turning to the *Tools to Boost Your Grade* section.

Standard GCSE (not IGCSE)

The section on your *Controlled Assessments* (starting on pg. 19) will give you more information on the writing component of your exam.

Oral Examination

All Candidates

Rules

Before the exam:

- Prepare answers to questions (related to your task if you are doing standard GCSE or related to topics on your syllabus for IGCSE) before the oral exam. The best prepared students get the best marks. It is incredibly hard to come up with answers to questions spontaneously under the pressure of an exam. So, you must go through answers to questions before the exam itself. There is a list of virtually all possible questions for different topics on pg. 65.
- Prepare **opinions** and **reasons** for those opinions while you practise answering questions. Remember: justification is key.
- In this preparation, use the same techniques as demonstrated previously in the *Writing Examination* section, using both standard phrases and opinion phrases to boost your mark (starting on pg. 37).
- It is up to you how you prepare. You can either write down answers to the oral questions or simply mentally prepare them. However, it is essential that you repeat your answers over and over again speaking them to yourself (over the course of a few weeks) so that, when it comes to the real exam, you have answered questions similar to the ones you are being asked before and therefore know roughly what to say.

Tip: Use your phone or tablet to record yourself speaking answers and then listen to your responses. This way, you will hopefully be able to spot some of the mistakes you make. Furthermore, the act of listening to yourself speaking is proven to help you remember information. So, answering questions will become easier the more you:

- Practise answering possible questions
- Listen to yourself

If there are words you find particularly difficult to pronounce, ask your teacher if he / she would mind you recording him / her saying these words for you to listen to and then say yourself.

- Make this preparation part of your routine as you do not need to be sat at a desk to do it! You could do it each evening, or while you are in the shower, or walking to school - whenever suits you, but just make sure you do it!

IGCSE Only

You will have to do a short presentation, followed by a couple of minutes of conversation based on the topic you have chosen for your presentation. There will then be 2 more conversations of roughly 3 minutes, each of them broadly about 1 of the following topic areas: Personal Relationships; Holidays & Tourism; Your Area & The Modern World; Leisure; Home Life; School & Work Life. (There is a list of virtually every possible question for these topics starting on pg. 65.)

As said above, it is up to you how you choose to prepare. However, we would advise preparing a few things which you can use for virtually any topic area:

- A description of a film. Say what it is about and why you liked it. This can be used if asked: What did you do on holiday? (*I went to see a film called... It was about...*) What did you do last weekend? What do you do in your free time? What did you do for your birthday last year?

Tip: It is quite hard to describe a film, so maybe look for a synopsis in German online, go through it with your teacher so that you understand everything, and then edit it so that it is not too long and it is in your own words. Add in your opinion of the film and reasons why you liked or disliked it at the end. (We are not encouraging plagiarism - that is wrong - but finding something online and then editing it to be your own is fine!) One of us did *Drachenzähmen leicht gemacht* or *How to Train Your Dragon*... And notice the use of the German title for the film, not the English one; this is far more impressive.

- A description of a book. Say what it is about and why you liked it. (One of us did *Per Anhalter durch die Galaxis* or *The Hitchhiker's Guide to the Galaxy*.)

All Candidates

During the exam:

Sustain and expand on the answers you give. So, for example, the two following conversations are from two different candidates in their English oral:

Oral Conversation 1:
Examiner: "So, where do you normally go on holiday?"
Candidate 1: "I normally go to Spain."
Examiner: "Why do you go there?"
Candidate 1: "Because Spain is pretty and the weather is nice."
Examiner: "Where did you go last year?"
Candidate 1: "Germany."
Examiner: "Did you enjoy it?"
Candidate 1: "Yes."
Examiner: "So, where are you going to go next year?"
Candidate 1: "I am going to go to Spain with my family."
Examiner: "What are you going to do?"
Candidate 1: "Relax on the beach."
Examiner: "Anything else?"
Candidate 1: "Yeah, I'd like to read and would like to visit Barcelona."
Examiner: "Oh, how come?"
Candidate 1: "I'd love to see Gaudi's architecture."

Oral Conversation 2:
Examiner: "So, where do you normally go on holiday?"
Candidate 2: "I tend to go to Spain with my family because I think that it is very pretty and the weather is normally terrific. However, last year I decided to go to Germany with my friends and we had a great time because there were loads of things to do."
Examiner: "Where are you going to go next year?"
Candidate 2: "I am planning on going to Spain with my family, and I hope that the weather will be good because I would love to spend a week relaxing on the beach. I will spend lots of time reading and I will visit Barcelona because I've always dreamt of seeing Gaudi's architecture."

Which conversation is more impressive? Well, Oral Conversation 2 would definitely score far more marks than the first one, **BUT** both these candidates know virtually the same amount of English (ok, the second knows slightly more vocab and a few neat phrases, but not that much more). So, the key here is to speak as much as possible. The questions from the examiner are there to prompt you as to what to say, not to trick you. You can tell how well your exam is going by how much the examiner speaks: the less the examiner speaks, the better.

However, stay on topic. For the holiday example above, don't start talking about your school because this will lose you marks for **Communication**.

The key is to be prepared but, during the exam, to sound like what you are saying is completely spontaneous and that you are simply making it up as you go along (when of course you are not). This can be done by:

- Throwing in a few *umms* and *ahhhs*, to make it seem as if you are not just recalling a prepared answer, but actually speaking. It is essential you sound spontaneous! Equally, it is important that you do not have too many long pauses in which you say nothing. Therefore, instead of sitting there *umming* and *ahhing* for ages when you are struggling to think of what to say, use ***also*** (equivalent to saying *well...* or *so...* in English, *alors* in French or *allora* in Italian) to give yourself time to think.
- Trying to change your intonation (not ridiculously) throughout your conversation so that you don't sound like your most boring teacher.
- Not being embarrassed to try and use a German accent. There are marks on offer for your accent, and even if your accent is not brilliant, it is better than speaking German in a plain English accent. The examiner will be happy just because you are giving it a go. On the contrary, when you can't be bothered to even make an attempt at an accent and sound like a lost English tourist in Berlin looking for 'Die Brandenburg Gate' what impression do you think that gives?... First impressions do count, so at least try!

So, the Golden Rules for your oral exam:

GOLDEN RULE :
SAY WHAT YOU KNOW, DON'T SAY WHAT YOU DON'T KNOW

GOLDEN RULE :
BE PREPARED BUT SOUND SPONTANEOUS

GOLDEN RULE :
EXPAND YOUR ANSWERS

GOLDEN RULE :
BREATHE SLOWLY AND REMEMBER THAT EVERYONE IS NERVOUS BEFORE THEIR ORAL!

Standard GCSE (not IGCSE)

Controlled Assessments: Writing & Oral Exams

You are lucky in comparison with people doing IGCSE. You are allowed to:

- Find out the precise title(s) of your essay(s) and oral conversation before your exam
- Plan your essay(s) and your oral in preparation for your exam
- Use a dictionary

The first thing to say is that the precise details of what you will have to do both in preparation for your tasks and in the tasks themselves will vary depending on which exam board your school uses for German GCSE. Most of you will have to write **two essays** and have **one oral conversation**. All three of these tasks need to be on **different topics**. The essays will each need to be around 250 words long. (However, you must confirm the exact details with your teacher.)

Writing

So, once you have found out the title(s) of your essay(s) (from now on we shall presume you will be writing two, but if not just adapt the system for one), you will need to stick to the following procedure in order to achieve the best possible marks.

Find out essay titles | Write essays in own time | Produce plans and teacher feedback | Learn essays | Nail the exam!

When writing your essays, you will be able to use:

- The material your teacher has given you on each of the topics covered in your two essays
- The material given in this book

This combination will help you to produce the best possible essays. They both need to be at the top end of the word limit, but remember not to go over it! All of the advice for the writing exam in the previous section applies here and is still crucial.

Once you have finished writing your essays, you need to produce a plan (the number of words allowed on this will depend on your exam board so ask your teacher) which you will be allowed to take into the exam room. Most exam boards also allow a few diagrams. It is up to you what you choose to write, but we would advise you to pick key words from each sentence which will remind you what the rest of the sentence should be, along with a diagram to tell you what each paragraph should be about.

Note: Most exam boards will not allow you to include conjugated verbs in your plan, so you must put particular emphasis on learning exactly how the verbs you will be using in your essays (and your oral) conjugate.

For example, if one of our sentences were:

Ich mag es mit meinen Freunden ins Kino zu gehen, weil ich dabei der Realität entkommen kann. - I like to go to the cinema with my friends because I can escape the real world.

We would include the following words in the plan:

Kino, Freunden, entkommen

Once you have completed your two essays and your two plans, your teacher will check through your plans and it will be up to you to make sure you learn your essays thoroughly. Then, all you have to do is copy them out in the exam room from your memory (with your plans to help you) and you are sorted!

We know that this sounds like an awful lot of work, but it really does produce the results you are after. We cannot guarantee anything, but we managed to get top A*s in Italian GCSE after just 8 months of studying the language using this technique. Trust us: when you get results like that, all of the hard work in preparation is worth it!

The last point to make is on the use of dictionaries. At the start we said that being able to use a dictionary was lucky... It is, but only if you use it properly.

Dictionaries should only have **two** uses in the examination room:

1. To **check** the **spelling** of any words included in your prepared essay which you are not 100% sure of as you write it out.
2. Very occasionally if there is a word which you know was included in your essay in English, but which you can't quite remember in German.

GOLDEN RULE :

DO NOT USE A DICTIONARY IN THE EXAM TO LOOK UP WORDS WHICH WERE NOT INCLUDED IN YOUR PREPARED ESSAY

If you have followed our system, there will be no need for this. Just remember the following Golden Rule when you are preparing your essays and when you are writing them out in the exam room:

GOLDEN RULE :

WRITE WHAT YOU KNOW, DON'T WRITE WHAT YOU DON'T KNOW

You will make sure you do this by using the information in your notes and in this book while writing your essays initially, only using a dictionary (can be online) to look up the occasional word.

Oral

The oral exam is in fact very similar to the writing exam. You will know the precise topic area of your oral conversation before the exam itself, so (using the questions on pg. 65 and any information your teacher may give you) you need to prepare answers to questions which you could possibly be asked. Once you have done this - either mentally or writing them down - you need to become familiar with your answers so that you can use parts of what you have prepared in the exam itself.

That's all there is to it really. All of the previous advice for both the oral and writing exams still applies when you are preparing for and taking your controlled assessments, so make sure you follow it!

Reading Examination

All Candidates

This about reading tell you boost at GCSE with easy steps. Don't worry; we know this is not good English (in fact there are 10 words missing). The point is that you don't need every detail to understand something. In your reading examination, you are **NOT** expected to understand every word. It is a test of your comprehension as well as your knowledge of German, so **DO NOT PANIC!** Use the words you understand to work out what the passage is about, and use clues such as the title or the questions in response to the passage in order to deduce what is going on. Here is a sample passage, which could be a text from a German GCSE Paper. There are no questions, but there are notes on how to establish what the article is about.

Ein gesundes Leben: haben Jugendliche schon zu viel zu tun?
Montag 8. September 2014

Allen Schülern und Schülerinnen wird gelehrt, dass Sport ein unentbehrlicher Teil des gesunden Lebens ist. Ob Sport tatsächlich so toll ist oder doch eher Mord, wie gerne behauptet wird, ist wohl Ansichtssache. Jedoch sagen Lehrer auch, dass es eine Notwendigkeit gebe, schlechtes Essen zu vermeiden. Es ist anerkannt, dass das Schulleben äußerst hektisch sein kann. Deshalb muss man fragen, ob man zu viel von Jugendlichen erwartet.

Markus Biedermann (16) ist Schüler am Dunkelwald-Gymnasium in Leipzig. Er will nächstes Jahr Abitur machen und möchte dann Medizin studieren.

„Zurzeit gefällt es mir nicht so gut in der Schule. Ich finde mein Leben ziemlich stressig. Jeden Morgen wache ich um zirka fünf Uhr dreißig auf, um meine Hausaufgaben zu machen, weil ich mich morgens viel besser konzentrieren kann. Wenn ich eine Dusche haben will, muss ich früher aufstehen! Ich habe fast keine Freizeit."

Markus braucht einen sehr hohen Notendurchschnitt, um Medizin studieren zu können. Deshalb steht er ganz schön unter Stress. „Ich fühle, dass viele meiner Lehrer im Großen und Ganzen tolerant sind, obwohl es natürlich manche gibt, die nicht verstehen können, wie viel ich machen muss. Sie geben mir keinen Raum zum Atmen."

Leider gibt es keine Kantine in der Schule, was bedeutet, dass Markus Essen in der Stadt finden muss, und zwar schnell, weil Markus' Eltern wollen, dass er nachmittags auf seine kleinen Brüder aufpasst. Das ist für ihn ein „ziemlich anstrengender" Nebenjob, aber wenn er sich entscheiden würde, die Wünsche seiner Eltern abzulehnen, bekäme er kein Taschengeld. Fastfood ist deshalb ganz sinnvoll. Jedoch kann Markus es nicht leiden. „Immer nur fettige Burger und Pommes – nein danke. Das ist nichts für mich! Ich stehe mehr auf Salate und frisches Gemüse, und ich trinke auch ziemlich gern frisch gepresste Fruchtsäfte." Deswegen hat er mehrere kleine Mahlzeiten. Zum Beispiel isst er etwas in der Pause um elf Uhr.

Obwohl seine Ernährung gesund ist, findet Markus Zeit für Sport nur am Wochenende, wenn seine Eltern nicht arbeiten müssen. Laut seinen Lehrern sollte er sich mindestens viermal pro Woche bewegen, aber klar ist, dass das unmöglich wäre.

Für Markus ist das ein sehr langer Tag. Er entspannt sich abends oft bei klassischer Musik oder mit einem heißen Bad, und er kriecht normalerweise zwischen elf und halb zwölf ins Bett. Es kommt darauf an, ob er ein gutes Buch zum Lesen finden kann oder nicht.

Key Points to look for in Reading Exam Questions

Title

The title will give you an instant idea of what the article is about. Here, the title is clearly a question, so we can be pretty certain the article will be answering that question. You should know that *Jugendliche* are *young people* - this is very basic vocabulary. We can then see that it is a question about healthy living (*gesundes Leben*), and about whether young people have too much to do already (*schon zu viel zu tun*). Hopefully you know all these words - if you don't, learn them! They're all pretty simple, but you might get something more complex that you've never seen before. Don't panic! You may be able to work it out from what it looks like or from the passage.

English Words

The highlighting on the next page shows all the words which we can work out purely from knowing English. From this alone, we can deduce most of what is being said in the passage. (If you didn't have a clue the first time you read it through, read it again once you have finished this page, paying close attention to the highlighting.) We would advise doing this in your exam: whilst you are reading through the passage, highlight or underline any words which are obvious to you from your knowledge of English, even if you haven't ever seen them before in German.

Furthermore, use other languages you may study to help you work out what words mean if you do not recognise them. E.g. If you do French, *une douche* means *a shower*... therefore, you can work out what *eine Dusche* means in German (*a shower*)!

Read Questions Then Text

Always read the questions **before you read the text** as these will give you a clue as to the content of the passage. They will also make you aware of the information you need to look out for when you are reading the text. (We know there are no questions for the text above... We are just trying to show that even with a hard text and no questions you can still get the gist of it!)

Ein gesundes Leben: haben Jugendliche schon zu viel zu tun?
Montag 8. September 2014

Allen Schülern und Schülerinnen wird gelehrt, dass Sport ein unentbehrlicher Teil des gesunden Lebens ist. Ob Sport tatsächlich so toll ist oder doch eher Mord, wie gerne behauptet wird, ist wohl Ansichtssache. Jedoch sagen Lehrer auch, dass es eine Notwendigkeit gebe, schlechtes Essen zu vermeiden. Es ist anerkannt, dass das Schulleben äußerst hektisch sein kann. Deshalb muss man fragen, ob man zu viel von Jugendlichen erwartet.

Markus Biedermann (17) ist Schüler am Dunkelwald-Gymnasium in Leipzig. Er will nächstes Jahr Abitur machen und möchte dann Medizin studieren.

„Zurzeit gefällt es mir nicht so gut in der Schule. Ich finde mein Leben ziemlich stressig. Jeden Morgen wache ich um zirka fünf Uhr dreißig auf, um meine Hausaufgaben zu machen, weil ich mich morgens viel besser konzentrieren kann. Wenn ich eine Dusche haben will, muss ich früher aufstehen! Ich habe fast keine Freizeit."

Markus braucht einen sehr hohen Notendurchschnitt, um Medizin studieren zu können. Deshalb steht er ganz schön unter Stress. „Ich fühle, dass viele meiner Lehrer im Großen und Ganzen tolerant sind, obwohl es natürlich manche gibt, die nicht verstehen können, wie viel ich machen muss. Sie geben mir keinen Raum zum Atmen."

Leider gibt es keine Kantine in der Schule, was bedeutet, dass Markus Essen in der Stadt finden muss, und zwar schnell, weil Markus' Eltern wollen, dass er nachmittags auf seine kleinen Brüder aufpasst. Das ist für ihn ein „ziemlich anstrengender" Nebenjob, aber wenn er sich entscheiden würde, die Wünsche seiner Eltern abzulehnen, bekäme er kein Taschengeld. Fastfood ist deshalb ganz sinnvoll. Jedoch kann Markus es nicht leiden. „Immer nur fettige Burger und Pommes – nein danke. Das ist nichts für mich! Ich stehe mehr auf Salate und frisches Gemüse, und ich trinke auch ziemlich gern frisch gepresste Fruchtsäfte." Deswegen hat er mehrere kleine Mahlzeiten. Zum Beispiel isst er etwas in der Pause um elf Uhr.

Obwohl seine Ernährung gesund ist, findet Markus Zeit für Sport nur am Wochenende, wenn seine Eltern nicht arbeiten müssen. Laut seinen Lehrern sollte er sich mindestens viermal pro Woche bewegen, aber klar ist, dass das unmöglich wäre.

Für Markus ist das ein sehr langer Tag. Er entspannt sich abends oft bei klassischer Musik oder mit einem heißen Bad, und er kriecht normalerweise zwischen elf und halb zwölf ins Bett. Es kommt darauf an, ob er ein gutes Buch zum Lesen finden kann oder nicht.

So, using what we have said, here is the general idea of each paragraph. You could work this out without us. (Honestly, we know the passage seems complicated, but when you spend time thinking about it and use the three key points on pg. 24, it's really not too bad!)

Paragraph 1: We can see that sport is being connected to young people - if we spot that *gelehrt* looks a bit like *Lehrer*, we can say that the schoolchildren are being taught that sport is an *unentbehrlicher* part of healthy living. You should know that *unentbehrlich* means *indispensable* or *essential* (– use it in an essay instead of repeating *wichtig* all the time!).

The next sentence is perhaps the hardest of the text - and is probably there to freak you out! *Ob...oder* simply means *whether...or*, so sport is either *great* (*toll*) or *Mord*, which actually means *murder*, but, if we don't know that, we can see it's a noun - and therefore the important bit - from the capital letter. (*doch eher* is just filling and means *rather* or *actually*.) If we skip to the end of the sentence, we can see a long word: *Ansichtssache*. We should be thinking: 'long word... probably made up of smaller bits'... and it is! *Ansichtssache* is a '*Sache of Ansicht*' or a '*thing of view*'... or a *matter of opinion*. Yes, this is tough to work out, but it's not impossible.

*However, teachers are also saying that ... bad food to *something**. Teachers are unlikely to be promoting the eating of unhealthy food. In fact, they're saying there's a *necessity* to *avoid* it. With **Not***wendigkeit*, think that the **Not***dienste* are the *emergency services* and that they are <u>necessary</u> services!

We can see then that *school life can be extremely (äußerst) hectic* and *we have to ask whether we expect too much of young people.* (You should see the *wartet* bit in *erwartet* comes from *warten* (*to wait*), and if you're waiting for something, it's not too much of a leap to say you're expecting it! Of course, you can just learn it! *erwarten – to expect*)

Paragraph 2: After the introduction, we can see that the text is moving on to an example. Markus is a 17-year-old school boy, who goes to a *Gymnasium*, which is a bit like a grammar school (not a gym!), in Leipzig. He wants to do the *Abitur* (like A Levels) next year, before studying medicine. That wasn't so bad, was it?

Paragraph 3: Notice that there are speech marks („ and " in German) and we're going into the first person. This tells us that Markus is speaking. You should know that *das gefällt mir* means *I like it*, so we can see that he's not having a great time in school. (Beware of negatives!) He's finding his life quite (*ziemlich*) stressful. He then talks about his morning routine, saying he gets up early for his homework - even earlier if he wants a shower. (*zirka* means *about*, i.e. not exactly 05:30.) He says he has *almost no free time*. (Words like *fast* (*almost*) are mark-losers, because they're small and people forget about them. Find a list on pg. 80.)

Paragraph 4: The text states that Markus needs a *very high Notendurchschnitt in order to be able to study medicine.* You should know that *Noten* are *marks* (as in "You scored 99%... What happened to the other 1%?!"). A *durchschnitt* is a *'through-cut'*, or in better English an *average*. Markus must boost his average mark. So, of course he's *under stress.* Lots of his teachers are *im Großen und Ganzen* (*on the whole*) *tolerant*, but there are *natürlich* (*of course* or *naturally*) some who don't understand how much he has to do. They give him *no room to breathe.* Notice how German constructions often look very similar to the English.

Paragraph 5: The text then changes direction a bit and moves onto Markus's diet, given that there is no canteen at the school. *und zwar* just means *and what's more* - it adds detail to what's already been said. We find out about the part-time job his parents give him: looking after his younger brothers in the afternoon. He doesn't have time to hang around, but he tells us that he *can't stand fast food* (n.b. *Pommes* are *chips*, not *apples*, if you're thinking French...) and prefers all that healthy stuff. *For that reason* (*deswegen* is *wegen* and the genitive of *das* i.e. *because of that*), he has several small *meals - mahl* looks a bit like *meal* (we know we're talking about food here!) and Zeiten are *times*, so, literally, *mealtimes.*
In the middle of all that, though, is a complex-looking conditional phrase: *if he decided to refuse his parents' wishes, he would get no pocket money.* The best thing to look at here is the separable verb *ablehnen* (which has split up for the *zu*). (The prefixes on German verbs often tell you something about their English translation: *ein-* for *in* or *into* (*einatmen* – *breathe in* or *inhale*), *weiter-* for the sense of continuing and *ab-* for *away* or *down* as in *ablehnen* – *push away* or *reject.*)

Paragraph 6: *Although* (*obwohl*) his *nutrition* is all well and good, it's *only at the weekend* (*nur am Wochenende*) that *he finds time for sport. According to* (*laut*) *his teachers he should exercise* (*bewegen* literally means *move*, so *sich bewegen* – *move oneself*) *four times a week, but it's clear that that would be impossible.* (Just as in English, the *un-* prefix normally makes something negative or the reverse.)

Paragraph 7: Given that *spannend* means exciting, *entspannend* means relaxing, so the verb is therefore *sich entspannen* (literally *to relax oneself*). Don't forget that *halb zwölf* actually means *half eleven* or 11:30 - it's halfway <u>to</u> twelve. One more thing: e*s kommt darauf an, ob...oder*, meaning *it depends on whether...or,* is a great expression to use in your oral!

If you can see the kind of things we're looking out for, you will definitely be in a very strong position to answer any questions. Just remember this golden rule:

> **GOLDEN RULE :**
> **YOU WILL NOT UNDERSTAND EVERY WORD, BUT YOU DON'T NEED TO**

So, up until now, this section has dealt with getting the gist of the hardest passages on the reading examination paper. However, you still have the task of answering the questions which accompany these passages. In all (I)GCSE examinations the majority of questions do not involve you writing in German, but instead include box ticking, English responses and multiple choice style questions. Clearly, to answer these questions, all you have to do is understand what both the passage and the questions mean.

Having said this, **examiners will try to trick you...**

...Therefore, there will always be a few questions in both the reading and listening papers designed to do just that. Examiners trick students by giving them two or more pieces of information to answer a question, with the first piece of information either not the precise answer to the question or only a part of the information needed to get the right answer, so please be careful and look out for this! For example, if the text translated to:

Nowadays, children spend an average of 2 hours and 45 minutes a day watching TV, and that doesn't even include the half an hour they spend on the internet or playing video games...

And you had to tick one of the boxes below:

Every day, children are in front of a screen for...

- ☐ *Two hours and fifteen minutes*
- ☐ *Two hours and forty-five minutes*
- ☐ *Three hours and fifteen minutes*

...We can guarantee that around 60% of students would tick the second box because they saw this piece of information in the text and jumped to the immediate conclusion that this must be the answer, without paying attention or thinking about the second piece of information given. So, make sure you are part of the 40% of candidates who gets this type of question correct. Avoid falling into the examiners' traps every time and you will be taking a firm step towards boosting your grade.

Note: There are some more ways in which examiners will try to trick you (although these are more common in the listening paper) on pg. 34.

Writing Answers in German

There is, for most exam boards (you should check with your teacher whether your exam board requires you to do this), a question which involves writing answers in German. This section will give you the tools you need to make sure you are able do this.

This is supposed to be one of the most difficult tasks you have to complete in your entire (I)GCSE exam. If you can do this, you immediately put yourself into the top bracket of candidates. To be honest, it really isn't that hard if you know exactly what you have to do. The following system requires minimal German knowledge and will ensure you know the precise technique needed to gain as many marks as you possibly can.

Markus Biedermann (17) ist Schüler am Dunkelwald-Gymnasium in Leipzig. Er will nächstes Jahr Abitur machen und <u>möchte dann Medizin studieren</u>.

<u>Markus braucht einen sehr hohen Notendurchschnitt, um Medizin studieren zu können.</u> Deshalb steht er ganz schön unter Stress. „Ich fühle, dass viele meiner Lehrer im Großen und Ganzen tolerant sind, obwohl es natürlich manche gibt, die nicht verstehen können, wie viel ich machen muss. Sie geben mir keinen Raum zum Atmen."

Leider gibt es keine Kantine in der Schule, was bedeutet, dass Markus Essen in der Stadt finden muss, und zwar schnell, weil Markus' Eltern wollen, dass er nachmittags auf seine kleinen Brüder aufpasst. Das ist für ihn ein „ziemlich anstrengender" Nebenjob, aber wenn er sich entscheiden würde, die Wünsche seiner Eltern abzulehnen, bekäme er kein Taschengeld. Fastfood ist deshalb ganz sinnvoll. Jedoch kann Markus es nicht leiden. „Immer nur fettige Burger und Pommes – nein danke. Das ist nichts für mich! Ich stehe mehr auf Salate und frisches Gemüse, und <u>ich trinke auch ziemlich gern frisch gepresste Fruchtsäfte.</u>" Deswegen hat er mehrere kleine Mahlzeiten. Zum Beispiel isst er etwas in der Pause um elf Uhr.

We have already analysed the above text (here we have only included three paragraphs) to deduce its meaning. There were previously no questions to accompany the text. This should have proved to you that you can understand the **vast majority** of any (I)GCSE passage without many tools to help you. However - now that we've convinced you of that - we are going to give you a couple of questions which require answers from the text above, **in German**. (Ignore the highlighting and underlining for now.)

1) Hohe Noten sind natürlich wichtig, aber <u>aus welchem Grund will Markus besonders gute Noten</u>?

[1]

First of all we need to understand the question. In order to do this we use the same methods we used to get the gist of the whole article and look for German words which resemble English ones, and also consider what the question is likely to mean. We have highlighted the words which have obvious English meanings. Often questions will contain more information than you really need, so you must deduce which part of the question is really necessary: why does Markus need especially good marks? (It is underlined for you.) We then need to look near the beginning of the text, because we are answering the first question, and **questions will always be given in the order the answers appear in the passage**. The answer to this is underlined in the first paragraph in the box on pg. 30.

> **Tip:** We are only looking for one primary reason because the question only has one mark (indicated by [1]) available.

Once you have found all the information you need, the key to answering the question is to use a mixture of:

- Words from the text
- Words from the question
- Your own words

So, using the above highlighting, an answer which would gain the mark available for this question would be:

Markus möchte besonders gute Noten, weil er Medizin studieren will.

> **Note:** Very often students are worried about 'lifting' (i.e. copying directly) from the text and so try to change everything into their own words and in the process lose marks. Examiners do not expect you to rephrase *Medizin studieren*, so don't try to. Instead, do simple things like using *wollen* instead of *möchten* and vice versa. There are no marks on offer for the quality of language used in your answers; they just need to make sense!

2) Im Text lernen wir, was Markus gern isst. <u>Was sagt er darüber, welche Getränke er mag</u>?
[2]

If we do exactly the same as we did on the first question, we see that the question is essentially asking for what Markus likes to <u>drink</u>. A question like this is very misleading, because the first half is totally irrelevant! Read it carefully! The answer to this is again underlined in the text (on pg. 30), and you should notice that it is found **after** the answer to the first question.

> **Tip:** This time, we need to look for two details because the question is worth two marks (indicated by [2]).

Here we have an issue which we did not come across in the last question and which is incredibly common in (I)GCSE exams. We need to say which drinks *Markus* likes, but the article says what *I* like to drink, because it is Markus who is speaking. If you 'lift' the answer directly from the text you will get **no marks** because you are talking about which drinks *you* like, rather than those which *Markus* likes. We cannot reiterate enough how important the skill of being able to change the information you are given in the text into the person required by the question is. This is so crucial that it is one of our Golden Rules. If you aren't good at this, ask your teacher to practise it with you.

GOLDEN RULE :
KNOW HOW TO MANIPULATE INFORMATION IN THE TEXT
It is crucial your answer makes sense, and if you get this wrong it can be incredibly costly!

So, our answer to this question would be:

Markus trinkt frisch gepresste Fruchtsäfte ziemlich gern.

There would be one mark for *Fruchtsäfte* and another mark for *frisch gepresste*.

Easier Reading Examination Questions

We have now addressed every aspect of the harder questions which will appear in your reading exam, but what about the easier ones? These easier questions are effectively a basic vocabulary test. You simply need to know the kinds of words they are likely to test you on and to learn these. There is a list of the kind of basic vocabulary that they are likely to test you on starting on pg. 72. **These lists are by no means extensive vocab lists; you need to learn more than just these!** There is also advice on how to learn vocabulary on pg. 70.

Finally, make sure you obey the following two Golden Rules. Every year a handful of people drop down a grade or two by not following these rules, regardless of their ability. Please be careful and don't fall into these traps!

Advice contained in the *Listening Examination* section is also applicable here.

GOLDEN RULE :
ANSWER THE QUESTION IN THE RIGHT LANGUAGE AND IN THE RIGHT TENSE

If the question asks for answers in English, make sure you give them in English. If it asks for them in German, give them in German! Equally, make sure your answer is written in the tense required by the question. This will normally be the tense the question is written in. If you don't do both of these things, you could lose all of the marks available for an entire question.

GOLDEN RULE :
GIVE THE INFORMATION YOU ARE ASKED TO GIVE

If the question asks you to tick 5 boxes, tick 5 boxes. If you have ticked 4 and are not sure of the last one, take a calculated guess. BUT, most importantly, do not tick 6! If you do you will probably lose all of the marks for that question. Equally, you should not write more information than needed or hedge your bets and write two answers. Only the first answer will be marked and, all too often - as we were told by an examiner - students lose marks by writing an incorrect answer before the correct one.
Similarly, if you are asked: *What is Sammy's favourite toy?* make sure you do NOT write down what John's favourite toy is!

Listening Examination

All of the advice (particularly the Golden Rules) given in the previous *Reading Examination* and *Writing Answers in German* sections applies to the listening exam, so read from pg. 23 if you haven't already.

First of all, you must have read and understood all of the questions which will be answered in the passage you are about to listen to **before** the recording begins to play. You are given plenty of time at the start of the exam and in between passages, so make sure you know exactly what the questions are looking for **before** the passage even starts.

Tip: Underline key words in the questions **before** the passage starts to play. This way, you'll know what information you need to listen out for. Be aware that the passage will probably not use exactly the same word as in the question, so listen out for words with the same or a similar meaning.

But, be careful! Often questions will say something like:

1) Apart from hamburgers, what is Jimmy's favourite food?

It is not uncommon for examiners to see the answer *hamburgers*, because some candidates are not careful enough or simply don't bother to read the questions before the start of the passage. Therefore, when they see *favourite food*, and hear the word *hamburgers*, they just write that down in the heat of the moment and quickly rush onto the next question. This is foolish and you cannot afford to throw away easy marks like this!

Once the passage begins to play - as obvious as this may sound - ensure you listen! Make sure you aren't too busy writing down an answer to hear the next part of the passage; it may contain the answer to the next question.

Solution: Write down, next to the answer space, either in English or German, a clear note or word to remind you of the answer. You are given time at the end of each question and at the end of the exam to come back and change or insert any answers. It is better to have clues to the answers of all 5 parts of a question and get 3 correct, than to only hear 2 parts of the question, and so only score a maximum of 2 marks.

Make sure you listen out for words similar to English words and also for key words in the question. However, be wary that you may hear key words from the question, but the examiners are trying to catch you out using **negatives** and different **tenses**. Therefore, do not assume that the first word or phrase that you hear is the one you need for your answer. For example, if the question were:

    2)   How much pocket money does Tom receive each week?

… and you heard Tom say:

"Als ich jünger war, hat mir meine Mutter zehn Euro pro Woche gegeben, aber jetzt gibt sie mir zwanzig Euro pro Woche."

… it would be easy to think that the answer you need is *10 euros*, because that is the first piece of information you are given which relates to the question. In fact, the answer is *20 euros*.

Similarly, if the question were:

    3)   How does Jenifer get to school?

… and the passage said the following:

"Jenifer fährt nicht mit dem Auto in die Schule. Sie fährt mit dem Zug dorthin."

… many candidates would write that she goes by car, when in fact the answer is: *She goes by train*.

Finally, there is a list of crucial vocab for your listening exam starting on pg. 72 (they are the same lists as for the easy questions in the reading examination). **These lists are by no means extensive vocab lists; you need to learn more than just these.** However, at the start of the listening exam there will be a number of relatively easy sections where this vocab could come up, and if you want to succeed in the exam it is critical you score very well on these easier sections, so make sure you learn the vocab.

Section II

Tools To Boost Your Grade

Phrases

These phrases are organized into different categories for different time periods of your essay (i.e. past, present and future). You should have these pages open while you are writing any essay in German - at least for now. Remember that you need to show off your use of different tenses, so it is crucial that you use plenty of phrases from each time period over the course of your essay.

Although there are quite a few phrases here, when you have practised using them a couple of times, you should begin to familiarize yourself with the phrases you most like to use. Then, we would advise making your own list of your favourite ones, taking at least 3 phrases from each category. Learn these for your exams, having checked with your teacher that you have written them correctly.

After that, use these phrases either while preparing for assignments (for standard GCSE) or during the examination itself (for IGCSE).

[verb] = followed by any verb
[inf.]. = followed by the infinitive form
(e.g. to do = machen) of any verb
[pa.p.] = followed by a past participle
(e.g. done = gemacht)

[pr.p.] = followed by a present participle
(e.g. Playing with his friends, the boy...)
[gerund] = followed by a gerund
(e.g. Beim Rugbyspielen...)

[present] = followed by the present
[cond.] = followed by the conditional
(e.g. I would do)
[subj.] = followed by subjunctive II

[noun] = followed by any noun
[adj.] = followed by any adjective

Don't worry too much about why these are used in a particular phrase. Just make sure that when you use a phrase, you also use the correct part of speech. Be careful: German constructions don't always use the same parts of speech as English constructions.

Note: The *List of Useful...* section, starting on pg. 50, includes lists of each of the parts of speech you will use with these phrases.

Tip: Make sure you're careful of word order. If you can't remember whether something goes to the end or gets inverted, have a look from pg. 50-52.

Standard Phrases

Present

1) Ich muss / kann / will **[inf.]** – I have (must) / am able (can) / want **[inf.]**

    Ich muss / kann / will meinen schwarzen Mantel **tragen**, wenn ich ausgehe. – I have / am able / want **to wear** my black coat when I go out.

2) Ich versuche, ...zu **[inf.]** – I try **[inf.]**

    Ich versuche, früh **aufzu**stehen, aber das finde ich schwer. – I try **to get up** early, but I find that difficult.

Note: Here you can see that with a separable verb like *aufstehen*, the *zu* goes in between the separable bit and the normal bit of the verb. See pg. 101 if you're not sure what we mean.

3) Ich **[verb]** gern (...), weil... – I like **[inf.]** / **[pr.p.]** (...) because...

    Ich **spiele** gern Eishockey, weil das ausgezeichnet für die Gesundheit ist, und ich denke, dass es spannend ist. – I like **to play / playing** ice hockey because it is great for your health, and I think that it is exciting.

4) Ich habe Lust, (...) zu **[inf.]** – I would like **[inf.]** (...).

    Ich habe Lust, in die Schweiz zu **fahren**, weil ich die Berge sehen will. – I would like **to go** to Switzerland because I want to see the mountains.

5) Ich komme gut mit **[noun (DAT)]** aus. – I get on well with **[noun]**

Ich komme gut mit meiner **Schwester** aus, aber ich hasse meinen Bruder. – I get on well with my **sister**, but I hate my brother.

Note: With this one, we're looking for a noun in the dative case, because *mit* takes the dative. Notice how in the example there's an **r** at the end of *meiner*. That's just like the **n** at the end of *meinen*, but instead of being accusative and masculine, it's dative and feminine. See pg. 119 for info on cases.

6) Beim **[gerund]** – By **[pr.p.]**

Beim **Fußballspielen** habe ich mir das Bein gebrochen. – I broke my leg (by) **playing football**.

7) Es gibt **[noun (ACC)]** – There is / are **[noun]**

Es gibt ein **Jugendzentrum** in meiner Stadt. – There is a **youth centre** in my town.

Note: Remember that *es gibt* takes a noun in the accusative case. Have a look at pg. 119 for info on cases and pg. 143 for more versions of *es gibt*.

8) Seit **+ time expression (DAT) + [present]** – I have been **[pr.p.] + for +** **time expression**

Seit **neun Jahren spiele** ich Tennis. – I've been **playing** tennis for **nine years**.

9) Obwohl ich … **[verb], [verb]** … – Although I **[verb]** …, … **[verb]** …

Obwohl ich Höhenangst **habe**, **waren** die Achterbahnen aufregend. – Although I **am** afraid of heights, the roller-coasters **were** thrilling.

10) Ich fühle mich **[adj.]** – I feel **[adj.]**

Ich fühle mich heiter, weil dieses Buch so **faszinierend** ist. – I feel cheerful, because this book is so **fascinating**.

11) Ich muss sagen, dass... – I have to / must say that...

i) Ich muss sagen, dass sie die schönste Frau war, die ich je gesehen habe! – I must say that she was the most beautiful woman I've ever seen!
ii) Ich muss sagen, dass er der schönste Mann war, den ich je gesehen habe! – I must say that he was the most handsome man I've ever seen!

12) (Es gibt) eine Menge **[noun (GEN)]** – (There is / are) a lot / loads of **[noun]**

Note: The GEN in brackets means we're after a noun in the genitive case. Again, have a look at pg. 119 for info on cases.

i) Wir geben eine Menge **Geld** für Kleidung aus. – We spend a lot of **money** on clothes.
ii) Es ist wichtig zu sagen, dass es eine Menge **guter Sachen** in diesem Supermarkt gibt. – It is important to say that there are loads of **good things** in this supermarket.

13) ...,um ... zu **[inf.]** – ... in order **[inf.]** ...

Ich gehe in die Stadt, um Obst und Gemüse zu **kaufen**, weil es so wichtig ist, gesund zu bleiben. – I go into town **to buy** fruit and vegetables, because it is so important to stay healthy.

14) ...,ohne ... zu **[inf.]** – ... without **[pr.p.]** ...

Ohne meinen Eltern etwas zu **sagen**, bin ich mit meinen Freunden ausgegangen. – Without **saying** anything to my parents, I went out with my friends.

15) ...,statt ... zu **[inf.]** – ... instead of **[pr.p.]** ...

Ich will zu Hause bleiben, statt meine Tante zu **besuchen**. – I want to stay at home, instead of **visiting** my aunt.

Tip: When you're **at** home, you say *zu* Hause, but if you're **going** home, it's **nach** Hause: *Ich hasse die Schule. Ich gehe nach Hause.* (*I hate school; I'm going home.*)

Past

1) Ich habe mich entschieden, …zu **[inf.]** – I decided **[inf.]**

   Ich habe mich entschieden, einige Postkarten zu **kaufen**, weil ich sie an meine Familie schicken wollte. – I decided **to buy** some postcards because I wanted to send them to my family.

2) Ich habe **[noun]** getroffen / kennengelernt – I met **[noun]**

Tip: Don't use *mit* with *treffen* on its own. With *sich treffen* (i.e. when it's reflexive), you can use *mit*. However, if you met someone for the first time, use *kennenlernen*, a separable verb (see pg. 101).

   i) Ich habe meinen **Vater** im Flughafen getroffen. – I met my **Dad** at the airport.
   ii) Ich habe viele sexy **Mädchen** / **Jungen** im Urlaub kennengelernt. I met lots of sexy **girls** / **boys** on holiday.

3) Ich habe viel Zeit mit **[gerund]** zugebracht – I spent a lot of time **[pr.p.]**

Tip: Even though *Zeit* is feminine (*die Zeit*), don't be fooled into thinking it should be *viele Zeit*. When the noun is singular, use *viel*; when it's plural, use *viele. Einfach!*

   Ich habe viel Zeit mit dem **Lesen** neben dem See zugebracht. – I spent a lot of time **reading** near the lake.

Note: *die* See – the sea   *der* See – the lake

Tip: The next couple of phrases are probably better in the simple past than the perfect. Remember that the weather in the past is almost always in the simple past: *es war wolkig – it was cloudy.*

The other way of thinking about this is that *haben, sein* and the modals (as well as *geben* in *es gibt*) are generally put in the simple past, as opposed to the perfect.

4) Als ich jünger war, **[past]** – When I was younger, **[past]**

   Als ich jünger war, **gab** es weniger Hausaufgaben. – When I was younger, there **was** less homework.

5) Das Wetter war schön. – The weather was nice.

6) Ich war gerade dabei, ... zu **[inf.]**, als ... – I was (in the process of) **[pr.p.]** when...

   Ich war gerade dabei, die Straße zu **überqueren**, als ich die Räuberin gesehen habe. – I was **crossing** the road, when I saw the (female) robber.

7) Ich hatte keine Lust, ... zu **[inf.]** – I did not want **[inf.]**...

   Ich hatte keine Lust, auf die Party zu **gehen**. – I did not want **to go** to the party.

8) Ich hatte keine Zeit, ... zu **[inf.]** – I had no time **[inf.]**...

   Ich hatte keine Zeit, das Buch zu **lesen**. – I had no time **to read** the book.

9) Es war nicht möglich, ... zu **[inf.]** – It was not possible **[inf.]**...

   Es war nicht möglich, den Bundestag zu **sehen**. – It was not possible **to see** the Bundestag.

10) Es hatte keinen Zweck, ... zu **[inf.]** – There was no point (in) **[pr.p.]**...

    Es hatte keinen Zweck in die Stadt zu **fahren**. – There was no point **going** into town.

11) Es begann zu regen. – It began to rain.

12) Nachdem ich (…) **[pluperfect]** … – After I **[past]** (…), …

Note: See pg. 98 for when to use *haben* or *sein*. You must use the pluperfect tense with *nachdem* if you want your German to look good… which you do!

Nachdem wir im Stadtzentrum **angekommen waren**, sind wir ins Theater gegangen. – After we **(had) arrived** in the centre of town, we went to the theatre.

13) Bevor ich (…) **[past]** … – Before I **[past]** (…), … / Before **[pr.p.]** (…), …

Bevor wir ins Kino **gegangen sind**, hatten / haben wir uns entschieden, etwas zu essen. – Before **going** to the cinema, we decided to eat something.

14) Ich hatte / war gerade … **[pa.p.]** – I had just **[pa.p.]**

Ich hatte gerade das Haus **verlassen**, als ich bemerkt habe, dass ich meine Schlüssel vergessen hatte. – I had just **left** the house when I realised that I had forgotten my keys.

15) Ich habe erkannt, dass ich Recht hatte / dass ich mich geirrt hatte. – I realised that I was right / wrong.

<u>Future</u>

Note: In English and in other languages, such as French, you can express the future with *to go / aller: I am going to do something* and *je vais faire quelque chose*. However, this does not work in German! You can't say *ich gehe etwas machen*! Ouch!

1) Ich habe vor, ...zu **[inf.]** – I plan **[inf.]**

   Ich habe vor, dieses Wochenende meine Großeltern zu **besuchen**. – I plan **to visit** my grandparents this weekend.

2) Ich habe die Absicht, ...zu **[inf.]** – I intend **[inf.]**

   Ich habe die Absicht, in den Sommerferien mit meiner Familie in die Vereinigten Staaten zu **fahren**. – I intend **to go** to the U.S.A. with my family in the summer holidays.

3) Wenn **[present]** – When **[present]**

Note: ...We are aware that this is not really a phrase, but it is important to remember that when using *when* to signify a future event (e.g. *when I'm 18...*) you use the present tense in German, as in English.

   Wenn ich 18 Jahre alt **bin**, werde ich reicher als mein Bruder sein. – When **I'm** 18, I'll be richer than my brother.

4) Ich hoffe, dass... – I hope that...

   Ich hoffe, dass meine Noten dieses Jahr besser sind. – I hope that my grades are better this year.

Note: Forgotten how to do comparisons? Look at pg. 109.

Phrases with the Subjunctive

Note: This set of expressions involve the subjunctive II. Go to pg. 94 if you don't know how to form it.

1) Ich möchte **[inf.]** – I would like **[inf.]**

   Wenn ich 17 Jahre alt bin, möchte ich Autofahren **lernen**. – When I'm seventeen, I would like **to learn** to drive.

2) Ich würde sagen, dass... – I would say that...

   Ich würde sagen, dass es unentbehrlich ist, kein fettiges Essen zu essen. – I would say that it's essential not to eat fatty food.

3) Wenn ich viel(e) **[noun]** hätte, **[subj.]** – If I had lots of **[noun]**, **[cond.]**

   Wenn ich viel **Geld** hätte, **würde** ich mir das größte Haus **kaufen**, das ich finden könnte. – If I had lots of **money**, I **would buy** the biggest house I could find.

4) Es wäre mir lieber, wenn... **[subj.]** – I would prefer it if **[subj.]** / **[imperfect]**

   Es wäre mir lieber, wenn es keine Hausaufgaben **gäbe**. – I'd prefer it if there **were** no homework to do.

5) Man könnte... – You (in general) could...

   Man könnte die Umwelt durch Recyceln schützen. – You could protect the environment by recycling.

6) Man sollte... – You (in general) should...

   Man sollte den Eltern öfter helfen. – You should help your parents more often.

7) Ich hätte … **[inf.]** mögen – I would have liked to have **[pa.p.]**

Ich hätte das Rathaus **sehen** mögen, aber es gab nicht genug Zeit. – I would have liked to have **seen** the City Hall, but there wasn't enough time.

8) Ich hätte … **[inf.]** sollen – I should have **[pa.p.]**

Ich hätte mehr **machen** sollen, als ich in Deutschland war. – I should have **done** more when I was in Germany.

9) Ich hätte … **[inf.]** können – I could have **[pa.p.]** / I would have been able **[inf.]**

Ich hätte mit Klaus **ausgehen** können, wenn ich meiner Mutter bei der Gartenarbeit früher geholfen hätte. – I could have **gone out** with Klaus, if I had helped my mum with the gardening earlier.

Note: Again, see pg. 98 for when to use *haben* or *sein* as this applies when using the **following** expression.

Be careful with the previous phrases (7 to 9): even if you're using the infinitive of a *sein* verb, use the subjunctive of *haben* (*hätte*), as it's going with the modal, not that infinitive. Modals (*müssen, sollen, wollen*, etc.) take *haben*.

10) Wenn ich (…) **[pa.p.]** hätte / wäre, hätte / wäre ich (…) **[pa.p.]** – If I had **[pa.p.]**.., I would have **[pa.p.]**…

Wenn ich **gewusst** hätte, dass der Lehrer krank war, wäre ich nicht in die Schule **gegangen**. – If I had **known** that the teacher was ill, I wouldn't have **gone** to school.

Opinion Phrases

Present Opinions

1) Ich denke, dass es **[adj.]** ist, (…) zu **[inf.]** – I think that it is very **[adj.] [inf.]** (…)

   Ich denke, dass es sehr **wichtig** ist, Freizeit zu **haben**, weil Stress ein riesiges Problem ist. – I think that it is very **important to have** free time, because stress is a huge problem.

Tip: Replace *ich denke* with *ich glaube, ich meine* or *ich finde*, just so the examiner doesn't get bored! You can also say: *ich bin der Meinung, dass* (*I am of the opinion that*), but sometimes it sounds a little… much.

2) Ich finde ihn / sie **[adj.]** – I find him / her / it **[adj.]**

Note: Use *Ich finde das [adj.]* to mean *I find it [adj.]* when talking about a concept or the act of doing something, rather than a specific noun.

   Leider denke ich nicht, dass mein Onkel genug Zeit haben wird, uns zu besuchen. Ich finde ihn wirklich **lustig**. – Unfortunately, I don't think that my uncle will have enough time to visit us. I find him really **funny**.

Note: Whilst in French *Je ne pense pas que* (*I don't think that*) takes the subjunctive, don't be fooled into thinking that *Ich denke nicht, dass* needs anything more than an indicative (i.e. normal) verb!

3) Meiner Meinung nach ist es **[adj.]** , dass **[verb]**. – In my opinion, it's **[adj.]** that **[verb]**

   Meiner Meinung nach ist es **ausgezeichnet**, dass mein Bruder so viel **macht**, um die Umwelt zu schützen. – In my opinion, it's **excellent** that my brother **does** so much to protect the environment.

Tip: The following expressions work exactly like *meiner Meinung nach*: *meiner Ansicht nach, meines Erachtens, für mich*

4) Es macht mir viel Spaß. – It is a lot of fun.

Past Opinions

1) Was mir am besten gefallen hat, war, dass ich ... [inf.] konnte, weil... – What I liked the most was being able [inf.]... because...

   Was mir am besten gefallen hat, war, dass ich jeden Abend **feiern** konnte, weil ich sehr gern Zeit mit meinen Freunden verbringe. – What I liked the most was being able **to party** every night, because I love spending time with my friends.

2) Ich habe immer davon geträumt, (...) zu [inf.] – I have always dreamt of [pr.p.] (...)

   Ich möchte Astronaut werden, weil ich immer davon geträumt habe, an einer Expedition in den Weltraum **teil**zunehmen. – I would like to become an astronaut, because I've always dreamt of **taking part** in a space expedition.

3) i) Ich habe ihn / sie / es [adj.] gefunden – I found him / her / it [adj.]
   ii) Ich habe ihn / sie / es so [adj.] gefunden, dass... – I found him / her / it so [adj.] that ...

Note: Remember that if you're talking about a thing that is masculine or feminine in German (regardless of whether you say 'it' in English or not), you need to use *ihn / sie*. (e.g. *Ich mag die Tür. Ich mag **sie**.* - not *Ich mag **es**!*) Also, use *Ich habe das [adj.] gefunden* to mean *I found it [adj.]* when talking about a concept or the act of doing something, rather than a specific noun.

   i) Ich denke, dass das Gemälde, das ich gestern gesehen habe, sehr schön war. Ich habe es **atemberaubend** gefunden. – I think that the painting that I saw yesterday was very beautiful. I found it **breath-taking**.
   ii) Unser Besuch war toll. Ich habe ihn so **spannend** gefunden, dass ich jetzt jedes Jahr nach Deutschland fahren will. – Our trip was great. I found it so **exciting** that I now want to go to Germany every year.

4) Das hat mir sehr gut gefallen. – I really liked it.

5) Ich habe es wirklich genossen. – I really enjoyed it.

6) Es war ein Erlebnis, das ich nie vergessen werde. – It was an experience I'll never forget.

CROATIANS – One Acronym to Rule them All

This acronym is a brilliant way to remind you of the tools you should employ while writing any essay, in order to boost your grade. Each of the letters of *CROATIANS* represents a different element that is guaranteed to impress any examiner. This acronym is particularly useful if you have to write an unprepared essay in your exam because, by the nature of being under exam pressure, you are likely to forget some of the tools at your disposal if you do not have a reliable way of remembering what they are.

Connectives are a great way to link together your ideas and, crucially, to form longer, more complex sentences that illustrate your ability to expand your ideas.

Reasons are, as has been made clear before, crucial if you want to succeed. The words *weil* and *da* must appear throughout your essay.

Opinion Phrases can be found in the previous section, starting on pg. 47. These are a brilliant tool for showing off complex grammar and, more crucially, are necessary if you want to obtain the best possible mark for Communication.

Adjectives – not just the boring ones! Try to employ a range of adjectives in your essay that demonstrate a greater knowledge of vocabulary and that make you stand out from the rest.

Tenses are vital. You must know and be able to use at least the present, perfect, future and simple past. (See pg. 86 onwards for help on tenses.)

Intensifiers should be used as a way of supplementing adjectives and increasing the complexity of the language you use.

Adverbs of Time are an essential tool for illustrating to the examiner which part of the question you are answering.

Negatives increase the level of sophistication of your essay.

Standard Phrases can be found in the previous section, starting on pg. 38. These will enable you to show-off your knowledge of complex grammar in the knowledge that what you are writing is totally error-free!

List of Useful...

This section is designed to go alongside the previous sections, *Phrases* and *CROATIANS – One Acronym to Rule them All*, by providing you with some parts of speech you can use in phrases and many of the tools listed in *CROATIANS*.

Connectives & Reason Words

The following table is full of incredibly useful connecting words to help you create the long sentences required in order to achieve the highest **Use of language** mark. They will also allow you to link from one sentence to the next.

The word order for when these words start a new clause is colour-coded. There is also a word order section in this book on pg. 130.

Verb goes to the end   Invert the subject and verb   No inversion

Connectives & Reason Words	Meaning	Example
weil / da	because / since	Ich möchte Berlin besuchen, **weil / da** ich gehört habe, dass es viele fesselnde Kunstgalerien gibt.
aber	but	Ich wollte in die Stadt fahren, **aber** ich konnte nicht.
und	and	Ich habe das Haus verlassen, **und** ich habe Henrik gesehen.
deshalb	therefore	Die Lehrerin war fantastisch, und **deshalb** haben wir gute Noten bekommen.
dann / danach / später	then / after that / later	Ich habe einen Apfel gegessen und **dann / danach / später** habe ich Wasser getrunken.

außerdem / weiterhin / zudem / dazu	in addition / furthermore / moreover / additionally	Sie ist sehr intelligent und sympathisch. **Außerdem / Weiterhin / Zudem / Dazu** spielt sie Klavier und Gitarre.
als	when (for talking about a time in the past)	**Als** ich jünger war, habe ich viele Bücher gelesen.
jedoch	however	Ich schwimme gern. **Jedoch** ist das Schwimmbad heute leider geschlossen.
seit (+ DAT)	since (a time)	**Seit** 2002 / **Seit** vielen Jahren bin ich Arsenal-Fan.
seitdem	since then	**Seitdem** habe ich versucht, sie zu vergessen.
trotzdem	nevertheless	Ich komme nicht so gut mit meinem Bruder aus. **Trotzdem** müssen wir im selben Haus wohnen.
zuerst	first (of all) / firstly	**Zuerst** muss ich sagen, wie glücklich ich bin.
dennoch	nevertheless	Diese Aufgabe ist schwer. **Dennoch** muss ich sie lösen.
während	while	**Während** sie anmutig tanzt, singe ich.
	whereas	**Während** er Fußball mag, kann ich Sport nicht leiden.
was [mich] betrifft	as for [me] / as far as [I am] concerned	**Was mich betrifft**, ist klassische Musik das beste Musikgenre.

auch	also	**Auch** haben wir Tischtennis gespielt.
obwohl	although	**Obwohl** ich Spanien liebe, spreche ich kein Spanisch.
aus diesem Grund	for this / that reason	**Aus diesem Grund** habe ich keine Zeit, mit meinen Freunden auszugehen.
einerseits **andererseits**	on the one hand on the other hand	**Einerseits** ist dieser Plan fantastisch, **andererseits** ist es ein zu hohes Risiko ihn umzusetzen.
wenn	when, if	**Wenn** ich müde bin, gehe ich ins Bett.
denn	because	Ich lese diese faszinierende Buch, **denn** es ist wichtig zu wiederholen.

Note: Sorry to keep banging on about this, but it is so important: *weil* and *da* (or even *aus diesem Grund* or *denn* to liven things up) should be used regularly throughout your essays because you should be giving:

- Justifications for why you did things
- What you thought of the things you did
- Why you have that opinion

Tip: Avoid using the connector *also* because it often has a different use to the word *so* in English, and it doesn't mean what it looks like! It is important to get it right if you do use it. As an alternative, use *deshalb* for *therefore / so*, and *außerdem / auch* for *in addition / also*. (That said, it can help you sound more authentic if you use it as a 'filler word' - an alternative to 'erm' and 'um' - like *alors* in French and *allora* in Italian.)

Adjectives

Remember that all these adjectives (and any you look up) are given as a 'stem' - you may need to add endings onto this basic form. Ensure you make them agree with the noun they are describing, but only if they come immediately in front of that noun. Agreements will be in gender (masculine / feminine), number (singular / plural) and case (nominative / accusative / genitive / dative).

Paula ist eine interessant**e** Frau. **BUT** Paula ist interessant.

Find the adjective endings that you need from pg. 106.

Feelings, Emotions & Opinions

deprimiert – depressed
entspannend – relaxing
froh – glad
gesund – healthy
glücklich – happy

krank – ill
lustig – funny
müde – tired
traurig – sad
zufrieden – satisfied , pleased

Overused Opinions

Some adjectives used to express opinion are overused and unimpressive to examiners. Sometimes, a particular word (even if it's a bit unimpressive) has to be used in order to get across the intended meaning. However, if another makes sense, replace the more boring word with one of these:

interessant – interesting
attraktiv – appealing
beeindruckend – impressive
charmant – charming
fesselnd – captivating
pädagogisch – educational

gut – good
angenehm – pleasant
ausgezeichnet – excellent
erstaunlich – astonishing
fabelhaft – fabulous
fantastisch – fantastic
genial – awesome
hervorragend – brilliant
sensationell – sensational

schlecht – bad
ekelhaft – disgusting
entsetzlich – appalling
furchtbar – awful
morsch – rotten
schrecklich – dreadful

langweilig – boring
ärgerlich – annoying
monoton – monotonous
stinklangweilig – deadly boring

Intensifiers

sehr – very
zu – too
viel – a lot , much
viele – a lot , many

ziemlich – quite
ein bisschen – a bit
wirklich – really
besonders – particularly

Note: Probably the most obvious intensifier in English is *more*. With German nouns you can use *mehr* (e.g. *mehr Geld*), but with adjectives and adverbs, things work differently. See pg. 109.

Adverbs of Time

immer – always
jeden Tag – every day
oft – often
häufig – frequently
normalerweise – normally
manchmal – sometimes

von Zeit zu Zeit – from time to time , every now and then
selten – rarely
nie – never
dann – then
danach – afterwards

More Adverbs of Time

At the moment (From now)		In the past (Looking back)	
vorgestern	the day before yesterday	**zwei Tage zuvor**	two days before
gestern	yesterday	**am Tag zuvor**	the day before
heute	today	**an diesem Tag**	(on) that day
morgen	tomorrow	**am nächsten Tag , am folgenden Tag**	(on) the next / following day
übermorgen	the day after tomorrow	**zwei Tage später**	two days later

Time Expressions

Here is a list of 11 basic time expressions. You should always use these in essays and oral conversations to show the examiner whether you are talking about the past, present or future. When you start a sentence (or a clause) with these, remember to invert the verb. (See pg. 130.)

Past
- vor drei Monaten...
  – three months ago...
- letzte Woche...
  – last week...
- letztes Wochenende...
  – last weekend...
- letzten Sommer...
  – last summer...
- während **+ GEN**...
  – during...

Present
- heutzutage... – nowadays...
- jetzt... – now...
- derzeitig... – currently...

Future
- nächstes Jahr...
  – next year...
- wenn ich 18 Jahre alt bin...
  – when I'm 18...
- dieses Wochenende...
  – this weekend...

Note: *während* is basically a preposition here. It's followed by the genitive case... See pg. 119 for more on cases and pg. 121 for info about prepositions.

Negatives

There are a couple of Golden Nuggets about negatives on pg. 140.

nein	no
nicht	not
kein	not a
nicht mehr	no longer
nichts	nothing
nie	never
niemand	no-one
gar nicht	not at all
überhaupt nicht	not at all

Verbs

The table below contains some of the most common verbs in the German language. We have written out what are known as the 'principal parts' of the verb, as these will help you form any tense. You must know and be able to recognise **all** of these in the infinitive form, as well as in the basic tenses, if you want to maximise your chance of success. **Note:** takes *sein* (see pg. 98), modal (pg. 91).

infinitive	3rd person singular – present	1st person singular – simple past	past participle	English
arbeiten	arbeitet	arbeitete	gearbeitet	work
bleiben	bleibt	blieb	geblieben	stay
brauchen	braucht	brauchte	gebraucht	need
denken	denkt	dachte	gedacht	think
essen	isst	aß	gegessen	eat
fahren	fährt	fuhr	gefahren	go (drive)
geben	gibt	gab	gegeben	give
gehen	geht	ging	gegangen	go (walk)
haben	hat	hatte	gehabt	have
hören	hört	hörte	gehört	hear
kaufen	kauft	kaufte	gekauft	buy
kommen	kommt	kam	gekommen	come
können	kann	konnte	gekonnt	be able to
leben	lebt	lebte	gelebt	live
lesen	liest	las	gelesen	read
lieben	liebt	liebte	geliebt	love
machen	macht	machte	gemacht	do , make
mögen	mag	mochte	gemocht	like
müssen	muss	musste	gemusst	have to
nehmen	nimmt	nahm	genommen	take
schwimmen	schwimmt	schwamm	geschwommen	swim
sehen	sieht	sah	gesehen	see
sein	ist	war	gewesen	be
spielen	spielt	spielte	gespielt	play
sprechen	spricht	sprach	gesprochen	speak
stellen	stellt	stellte	gestellt	put , place
verlassen	verlässt	verließ	verlassen	leave
werden	wird	wurde	geworden	become
wohnen	wohnt	wohnte	gewohnt	live
wollen	will	wollte	gewollt	want to

Sentence Structure Formula

You hopefully remember that in order to boost your mark for **Use of language** you need to use longer sentences. This is true... **BUT** do not make them more than a few lines long or you will begin to make mistakes and they will become confusing.

So, what you need to do is: try to use a combination of phrases (often a standard phrase with an opinion phrase) in order to produce more complex sentences. You can then link these phrases and sentences together with time expressions and connecting words.

Here is an example of how this works:

Present phrase	Normalerweise fahre ich nach Frankreich,
um...zu	um Zeit mit meiner Familie zu verbringen,
weil / da	weil
Opinion phrase	es einfach ist, mit dem Schiff zu fahren,
Connecting words	und weil
Opinion phrase	wir denken, dass französisches Essen
Time expression	immer
Opinion phrase continued	toll schmeckt.

Clearly, the above is not a hard-and-fast structure which you have to use for every single sentence you write; evidently that would be ridiculous. However, it ought to give you an example of how you can string together plenty of the different structures we have shown you. We can tell you with absolute certainty that doing so correctly will greatly boost your mark in any (I)GCSE essay or oral examination. Using this idea, you ought to get into the habit of giving reasons for virtually everything you say by using a mixture of standard phrases, opinion phrases and the words *weil* or *da*.

Note: There is a section on word order starting on pg. 130.

Sample Essay Question

Here is a sample essay on holidays, packed full of great expressions. You will find a key to the colour coding at the bottom of the next page. The task / title is as follows:

You recently travelled to Germany on holiday. Write about your visit, including:

- *What you normally do for your holidays*
- *How you travelled to Germany*
- *What you saw and did as well as your opinion of German culture*
- *Where you will go on future holidays and why*

[1]**Normalerweise** fahre ich nach Frankreich, [6]**um** Zeit mit meiner Familie **zu** verbringen, [5]**weil** [4]**es einfach ist**, mit dem Schiff zu fahren, und [5]**weil** [4]**wir denken**, dass französisches Essen immer toll schmeckt. [4]**Meiner Ansicht nach** ist ein Urlaub mit der Familie ausgezeichnet, [5]**da** [6]**ich selbst nichts ausgeben muss**, [6]**auch wenn es keine Möglichkeit gibt**, mit meinen Freunden zu sprechen.

[1]**Normally** I go to France [6]**in order to** spend time with my family, [5]**because** [4]**it's easy to go by boat** and [5]**because** [4]**we think** that French food always tastes great. [4]**In my opinion** a family holiday is excellent, [5]**as** [6]**I, myself, don't have to spend anything**, [6]**even if there is no opportunity** to speak with my friends.

[2]**Letzten Sommer** bin ich mit meiner Freundin nach Berlin gefahren, [7]**und** wir haben viele angenehme Aktivitäten gefunden. Wir sind dorthin geflogen, [6]**statt** mit dem Zug **zu** fahren, [4]**was fantastisch war**, [5]**weil** [6]**der Flug nur zwei Stunden gedauert hat**, [6]**obwohl** [4]**ich das Essen absolut furchtbar fand**.

[2]**Last summer** I went to Berlin with my girlfriend [7]**and** we found lots of pleasant activities. We flew there, [6]**instead of** going by train, [4]**which was fantastic**, [5]**because** [6]**the flight only lasted two hours**, [6]**although** [4]**I found the food absolutely awful**.

[6]**Als es sonnig war**, [6]**sind wir in der Stadt spazieren gegangen**. [7]**Danach** haben wir den Fernsehturm besucht, [7]**von dem** wir die ganze Stadt sehen konnten. [5]**Wegen** des fantastischen Wetters [4]**war das meiner Meinung nach toll**. [4]**Was mir jedoch am besten gefallen hat**, war unser Besuch im Bundestag, [5]**weil** [6]**ich immer davon**

[6]**When it was sunny**, [6]**we went walking in town**. [7]**After that**, we visited the TV Tower, [7]**from which** we could see the whole city. [4]**In my opinion that was great**, [5]**because of** the fantastic weather. [4]**However, what pleased me the most** was our visit to the Bundestag, [5]**because** [6]**I have always**

geträumt habe, Politiker zu werden. **⁷Außerdem** haben wir das Brandenburger Tor gesehen, **⁴was für mich hervorragend war**, **⁵da** **⁶ich mich** für deutsche Architektur interessiere.

²Am folgenden Tag **⁶haben wir uns entschieden**, ein Museum für moderne und zeitgenössische Kunst zu besuchen, **⁷das** leider überfüllt war, und **⁷in dem** **⁶wir die Gelegenheit hatten**, viele seltsame Werke zu sehen. **⁶Trotz der Menschenmassen** war das **⁵dank** der faszinierenden Kunst und Kultur **⁴ein unvergessliches Erlebnis**.

⁴Wenn ich die Wahl **⁸hätte,** **⁸würde ich** **³nächstes Jahr** nach Amerika **fahren,** **⁵um** die Wolkenkratzer in New York **zu** sehen. **⁷Leider** **⁶haben** meine Eltern **vor**, dass die Familie bei meinen Großeltern bleibt, **⁷die** in Schottland wohnen. **⁴Ich hoffe, dass dieser Besuch nicht zu monoton sein wird**, und dass das Wetter **⁶so gut wie möglich** sein wird. **⁶Wenn ich älter bin,** werde ich in die Mongolei fliegen, **⁵weil** **⁴ich authentische asiatische Gerichte essen möchte**.

dreamed of becoming a politician. **⁷In addition**, we saw the Brandenburg Gate, **⁴which was brilliant for me**, **⁵since** **⁶I** am interested in German architecture.

²On the following day, **⁶we decided** to visit a modern and contemporary art museum, **⁷which** was unfortunately crowded, and **⁷in which** **⁶we had the opportunity** to see lots of peculiar works. **⁶Despite the crowds**, it was **⁴an unforgettable experience**, **⁵thanks** to the fascinating art and culture.

⁴If I **⁸had the choice, I** **⁸would** **go** to America **³next year** **⁵to** see the skyscrapers in New York. **⁷Unfortunately**, my parents **intend** that the family stay at my grandparents' house **⁷–** they live in Scotland. **⁴I hope that this visit won't be too boring** and that the weather will be **⁶as good as possible**. **⁶When I'm older,** I'll fly to Mongolia, **⁵because** **⁴I would like to eat authentic Asian cuisine**.

¹- Adverb of time shows you are answering the 1st bullet point in the present.
²- Adverbs of time show you are answering the 2nd & 3rd bullet points in the past.
³- Adverb of time shows you are answering the 4th bullet point in the future (and using subjunctive II).
⁴- Opinion phrase
⁵- Reason in order to explain why you have an opinion about something
⁶- Very natural 'standard' German phrase
⁷- Connecting word / Relative clause
⁸- Subjunctive... **MARKS!!**

Notice that throughout this sample essay, the spread of different colours is fairly even. Note the presence of:

- A mixture of standard phrases, opinion phrases and reasons for these opinions
- Plenty of connecting words and time expressions
- Subjunctives to really boost the **Use of language** mark

When you write essays, the key is to manipulate phrases to suit the essay title, just as we have done in this sample essay. Looking at the sample essay again, with the mark scheme (which gives marks for: **Communication**, **Use of language** and **Accuracy**) in mind, we can see that:

1. There are 5 paragraphs in response to the 4 bullet points (We split one bullet point into two parts). Tenses are used correctly throughout each paragraph. Each paragraph responds specifically to each part of the essay title. The essay is easy to understand and makes sense. Therefore, it will be awarded **full marks** for **Communication**.
2. There are plenty of constructions, all correctly used, which add fluidity to the essay. A couple of subjunctives are also thrown in! So, **full marks** for **Use of language**.
3. There are no spelling mistakes and there are no mistakes in the use of tenses. All verbs agree with their subjects (the thing doing the verb) and all adjectives agree with their nouns. (This was made easier by using the checking rule on the next page.) Therefore, it would be given **full marks** for **Accuracy**. Please be aware that, although there are no mistakes in this essay, you will be allowed to make some relatively small mistakes and still be awarded full - or close to full - marks for **Accuracy** in your exam. You are not expected to be perfect!

… Finally, we would like to emphasise the point we made right at the start of this guide: You do **not** (in reality) have to have done everything you write about in your essay. You will probably have noticed that this sample essay is about going on holiday to Berlin with *my girlfriend*. Neither of us have ever been cool enough to do that…! Our parents also aren't forcing either of us to visit grandparents in Scotland! The reason we included these was to make you realise and remember that your essay absolutely does not have to be factually correct… You **must** make it up to show off your use of German!

The Checking Rules

You now know how to boost your mark for **Communication** and **Use of language**, but how can you improve your **Accuracy** mark?

Unfortunately, unless you want to spend hours learning vocabulary lists, we cannot help you with your spelling. However, there is an essay checking formula which, once you have written an essay, should be used without exception. It is in **three parts**:

PART 1:

- Have your completed essay in front of you and take out a pencil.
- Underline each verb (word of doing) (e.g. *er spricht – he speaks*)... Make sure you don't miss one out!
- Now, go back to the top of the essay, to the first underlined verb.
- Ask yourself four questions about this verb:
    - What is the verb supposed to say in English? (e.g. *he speaks*)
    - What tense is the verb in, in English? (e.g. *he speaks* is present)
    - What person (I, you (sg. familiar), he / she / it, we, you (pl. familiar), they, you (polite)) is that verb, in English? (e.g. *he*)
    - What is the infinitive (i.e. the '*to*' form of the verb) in English, then in German? (e.g. *to speak – sprechen*)
    - Is this verb weak, strong or irregular? (Not sure what this means? Look at pg. 89 - e.g. *sprechen* is a strong verb and has a vowel change in the stem for two parts in the present tense.)

If you're using an irregular verb (e.g. *sein*), you must be certain about what the verb should look like for that tense, person and number (singular / plural)! The infinitive doesn't always tell you!	If the verb is weak or strong, you need to check the ending of the verb using your knowledge of verb conjugation. (e.g. *er* is 3rd person singular, which has a **-t** ending in the present tense.)

- Rub out the pencil under this verb and correct it if you were wrong.
- Repeat the process on every verb.

Note: For more explanation on the use of different tenses and how to construct them, have a look at the *Verbs* section which starts on pg. 85.

PART 2:

- Having completed Part 1, go back to the start of your essay and underline, in pencil, every adjective (descriptive word) (e.g. *fantastisch – fantastic*) that appears before a noun (a thing, an object, a person, etc.). Adjectives that appear after nouns (e.g. *Der Mann ist **glücklich**.*) do not agree with their noun. Carry out the following procedure on every word now underlined:

- Ask yourself: "What noun is this adjective describing?" (e.g. *eine Frau* or *ein Mann*)
  - o Is that noun masculine, feminine or neuter? (If you don't know what the gender of this noun is, just make an informed guess. Have a look at *The Rules of Sex* section on pg. 115 for help on working this out.)
  - o Is the noun singular or plural? (Is there one or more than one?)
  - o What case is the noun? (e.g. nominative) (Help can be found on pg. 119, if you've forgotten about the different cases)

- Using your answers to the questions above, work out what ending the adjective should have. Refer to the section that begins on pg. 106. The tables (which must be learnt!) start on pg. 107. Remember that endings change depending on what else comes in front of the noun. For instance, even though it's *der groß**e** Tisch*, it's *ein groß**er** Tisch* (and both of these are the same gender, number and case: masculine nominative singular!).

- Correct any mistakes you may have made in the agreement of that adjective and rub out the pencil mark under that word.

PART 3:

- You should also check the articles: words like 'the' and 'a'. As you know, there are loads of variations of *der*, *die* and *das*, and of *ein*, *eine*, *ein*.

- Apply the same sort of processes as in part 2, so that you can be sure that the gender, number and case are right for the noun that they go with.

Points to Remember for the Writing Exam

- **Be creative!** You can make up anything you want, as long as you know how to say it and it is relevant to the essay title.

- **Don't miss anything out!** Write a paragraph per bullet point or per part of the essay title (depending on the form in which the task / title is given to you).

- **Remember *CROATIANS*!**
  - **C**onnectives to form longer sentences.
  - **R**easons to justify why you have / had a certain opinion.
  - **O**pinion Phrases to express your thoughts.
  - **A**djectives – not just the boring ones!
  - **T**enses to answer each part of the question.
  - **I**ntensifiers to supplement adjectives.
  - **A**dverbs of Time to show which part of the question you are answering.
  - **N**egatives to increase the sophistication of your essay.
  - **S**tandard Phrases to show off your knowledge of complex grammar.

- **Sound German!** Use both standard phrases and opinion phrases, but make sure you don't force them.

- <u>**Always**</u> **justify!** Every time you give an opinion it must be justified with a reason.

- **Check your work!** Use the Checking Rules to make sure your work is as error-free as it can possibly be. Ensure you leave yourself enough time to do this and try imagining you are finding faults in your arch-nemesis's work!

YOU MAY NOT HAVE TO DO THIS. If your teacher has not told you about preparing a picture for your oral presentation, skip this page!

Oral Picture Presentation

Firstly, it is important that you choose a picture or photograph that is going to show off your knowledge and that makes the examiner's life easy by containing lots to talk about. We would recommend an image with plenty of action and people included in it. During your preparation, you should prepare a sentence or two to describe what each person or object is doing in the picture as well as a sentence about each person in general (e.g. their personality, hobbies etc.). This covers some of the starter questions the examiner is likely to ask you.

If you have to describe a photo in your oral examination (as your presentation), here are some phrases for describing a picture:

- Meine Mutter hat dieses Foto gemacht, als... – My mum took this photo when...
- Letztes Jahr... – Last year
- Bei einem Schulausflug – During a school trip
- Wie man sehen kann... – As you can see...
- Diese Szene fand [in Berlin] statt. – The scene took place [in Berlin].
- Mit mehreren Familienmitgliedern – With several members of my family
- Als wir eine Wohnung in Deutschland gemietet haben – When we rented an apartment in Germany
- Auf der linken Seite sieht man meinen Bruder... – On the left, we see my brother...

Position words to describe a photo:

- auf der linken Seite / links – on the left
- auf der rechten Seite / rechts – on the right
- in der Nähe von – near to
- im Vordergrund – in the foreground
- im Hintergrund – in the background
- neben **+ DAT** (see pg. 119 for info on cases) – next to

Oral Exam Questions by Topic Area

Here is a list of virtually every question you could be asked in your (I)GCSE examination. The questions are split up into different oral topic areas. If you are doing a standard GCSE, you should only prepare questions which are related to your task(s). However, for IGCSE, you may be asked any of these questions and so should prepare answers for most of them (**if they are on your syllabus**).

Topic Area I – Personal Relationships

Wie siehst du aus?
Sag mir etwas über deine Persönlichkeit?
Beschreib mir deine Familie.
Was sind die Vor- und Nachteile von Geschwistern?
Wie kommst du mit deiner Familie aus?
Was sind die Ursachen von Streitigkeiten zwischen dir und deinen Eltern?
Warum können ältere Menschen Jugendliche nicht verstehen?
Ist deine Familie wichtig deiner Meinung nach?
Sag mir etwas über deinen besten Freund / deine beste Freundin.
Was macht ihr zusammen?
Streitest du dich manchmal mit deinen Freunden? Warum?
Warum sind Freunde wichtig?
Was sind die Eigenschaften eines guten Freunds / einer guten Freundin?
Was hast du letztes Wochenende mit deinen Freunden gemacht?
Was sind die größten Probleme, die du hast?

Topic Area II – Holidays & Tourism

Reist du gern? Warum?
Hast du ein anderes Land besucht? Welches?
Was hast du gemacht? War diese Reise gut?
Was hast du über das Essen gedacht?
Wohin fährst du lieber?
Bleibst du lieber in einem Hotel oder in einem Zelt?
Welche Länder möchtest du besuchen?
In England bleiben oder ins Ausland fahren: was meinst du? Warum?
Bist du nach Deutschland gefahren? Sag mir etwas über deine Reise...
Was sind die Unterschiede zwischen dem Leben in Deutschland und in England?
Wie wirst du deinen Urlaub dieses Jahr verbringen?
Beschreib mir deinen idealen Urlaub.

Topic Area III – Your Area & The Modern World

Wohnst du in einer Stadt oder in einem Dorf?
Beschreib mir deine Stadt / dein Dorf.
Was können Jugendliche dort tun?
Gibt es etwas Interessantes in deiner Gegend zu tun?
Was gibt es für Touristen in deiner Gegend?
Was sind die Probleme in deiner Gegend?

Interessierst du dich für die Umwelt? Warum?
Was machst du, um die Umwelt zu schützen?
Machst du etwas in der Schule, um den Planeten zu retten?
Was ist deiner Meinung nach das größte Problem für die Umwelt?
Was sollte die Regierung machen?
Was wird geschehen, wenn man nichts tut?
Glaubst du, dass die Erderwärmung Probleme in der Zukunft in deinem Land verursachen wird? Was für Probleme sind das?

Sind die Nachrichten wichtig für dich? Warum?
Was passiert heute in deinem Land?
Was denkst du über Werbung?
Hast du ein Handy? Glaubst du, dass junge Leute von ihren Handys besessen geworden sind?
Was sind die Vor- und Nachteile von Handys?
Sind Computer deiner Ansicht nach nützlich?
Was wird die Aufgabe von Computern in der Zukunft sein?
Benutzt du oft das Internet?

Topic Area IV – Leisure

Was sind deine Hobbys?
Bist du sportlich?
Ist es wichtig, Sport zu treiben?
Gibt es Sportler, die Vorbilder für dich sind? Warum bewunderst du sie?
Was hast du letztes Wochenende gemacht?
Was wirst du heute Abend machen?
Was wirst du nächstes Wochenende machen?
Was hast du in den Osterferien gemacht?
Spielst du ein Musikinstrument?
Was magst du für Musik?
Konzerte oder CDs?
Warum ist Musik wichtig für dich?

Was magst du für Filme?
Hast du kürzlich einen Film gesehen?
Hast du einen Lieblingsfilm?
Wer ist dein Lieblingsschauspieler / deine Lieblingsschauspielerin?
Siehst du oft fern?
Was ist deine Lieblingssendung?
Was sind die Vor- und Nachteile von Fernsehen?
Sehen junge Leute deiner Meinung nach zu viel fern?

Topic Area V – Home Life

Wo wohnst du?
Beschreib mir dein Haus / deine Wohnung.
Beschreib mir dein Zimmer.
Was machst du in deinem Zimmer?
Was machst du zu Hause, um deinen Eltern zu helfen?
Was machst du nicht so gern?
Wer kocht bei dir?
Beschreib mir dein ideales Haus.
Sag mir etwas über deine Tagesroutine.
Was hast du gestern gegessen?
Was isst du gern zum Frühstuck?
Was wirst du heute Abend essen?
Was ist dein Lieblingsessen?
Ernährst du dich ausgeglichen?
Was hältst du von Vegetariern?
Was sollte man machen, um fit / gesund zu bleiben?
Bist du fit?
Treibst du viel Sport?
Wie kann man Menschen ermutigen, mehr Sport zu treiben?
Sind Diäten gefährlich?
Rauchst du? Warum?
Warum fangen manche Jugendliche an zu rauchen?
Wie kann man Jugendliche entmutigen zu rauchen?
Trinkst du Alkohol? Warum?
Sind Drogen gefährlich?

Topic Area VI – School & Work Life

Sag mir etwas über deine Schule.
Welche Fächer lernst du in der Schule?
Was ist dein Lieblingsfach? Warum?
Gibt es ein Fach, das du überhaupt nicht magst?
Was sind die Vor- und Nachteile deiner Schule?
Wie viele Stunden hast du jeden Tag?
Was machst du in der Pause?
Isst du in der Kantine? Magst du das Essen?
Beschreib mir einen typischen Schultag.
Trägst du eine Schuluniform? Magst du sie?
Welche Sportarten treibst du in der Schule?
Gibt es gute Sporteinrichtungen?
Gibt es außerschulische Aktivitäten?
Bekommst du deiner Meinung nach eine gute Ausbildung?
Wie könnte man deine Schule verbessern?
Was hast du vor, im September zu lernen?
Wirst du (an der Universität) studieren? Warum?
Was willst du beruflich machen?
Wie bekommst du dein Taschengeld? Was musst du machen, um es zu verdienen?
Hast du einen Nebenjob?
Hast du ein Praktikum gemacht? War das ein interessantes Erlebnis?
Wo wirst du im Jahr 2030 sein?

Section III

Specific Essential Learning

Vocabulary

··

There are a few condensed vocab lists starting on pg. 72. These contain words which are likely to come up in the reading and listening papers, particularly in the first few sections. You must learn these lists thoroughly as all of this vocab is certainly expected of you at (I)GCSE. (However, this is not a guarantee that it will definitely come up!) It is also important that you realise that these lists are nowhere near exhaustive and that you must do your own vocab learning if you want to succeed in your German exams.

There is some essential vocab which you simply cannot do without. (Obviously you aren't going to understand anything without some core knowledge of the basics.) Beyond that, there are loads of fairly extensive vocab lists online or in GCSE vocab books. Regardless of which vocab lists you choose to use, we would advise you to go through the most important sections (such as topics you are likely to want to write an essay on or speak about in your oral), highlighting vocab you don't know. Then, follow our three Golden Rules for learning vocabulary:

GOLDEN RULE :
LEARN IT IN SMALL CHUNKS, BUT REGULARLY

Our advice is that you should learn just 4-7 words every day. Have a list of words which you want to learn on a sheet - print off a GCSE vocab list from your exam board, for example - and highlight all the ones you are not 100% certain of on one day. (This might take a bit of time - why not go and do it now?) Then, each day for around 10 minutes - perhaps while eating breakfast or before going to bed - learn 4-7 of those words (you decide exactly how many). Test yourself, and once you can remember the English translation of each German word, you're done for the day.

GOLDEN RULE :
COME UP WITH WAYS OF REMEMBERING WORDS

It's hard to just learn stuff which has no significance to you, for example a random list of words. Therefore, we use little sayings, which are really weird (**BUT** they work for us) to help us remember vocab. For example, *eine Ansiedlung* is *a settlement.* Try thinking about it this way: 'A settlement is where people planted themselves… like seeds!'

GOLDEN RULE :
REVISE VOCAB

Learning vocab can be incredibly dull, but it is vital. It is easy to become frustrated when you have learnt 5 words one day and then, within 3 days, have forgotten them completely. So, in the first Golden Rule, we said to learn 4-7 words a day, but you may forget the vast majority of the vocab within a week. Therefore, every 4 or 5 days, don't learn anything new. Instead, spend 10 minutes testing yourself on the vocab you have been learning over the past few days. Then, any words which you have forgotten - there will probably be a few - should be underlined and re-learnt as if they were new to you (as one of your 4-7 daily words).

All this might sound complicated, but it really isn't. Just spend a few minutes every day doing it and it will automatically become part of your routine. Just think how much you will learn from such a small amount of time every day: within a year you will have learnt at least 600 words.

Basic Vocab

Sportarten und Hobbys – Sports and Hobbies

Note: With the following words, you might be looking for a noun, but find a verb instead. With some of them, that's easy to change: *angeln* (*to fish*) becomes *das Angeln* (*fishing*). A verbal noun or a 'gerund'!

angeln	to fish
Basketball (m)	basketball
Bogenschießen (n)	archery
Eislaufen (n)	ice skating
Fußball (m)	football
Klettern (n)	rock climbing
Leichtathletik (f)	athletics
Pferd (n)	horse
Radfahren (n)	cycling
reiten	to ride (a horse)
Schach (n)	chess
schwimmen	to swim
Segelboot (n)	sailing boat
segeln	to sail
Skifahren (n)	skiing
spielen	to play
tanzen	to dance
Tennis (n)	tennis
Tischtennis (n)	table tennis
Wasserski (m)	water skiing

Note: In German, don't say *Sport spielen*, say *Sport treiben*. In English, it is acceptable to say *play sport*, but it's not something that's said in German. However, for the sports for which we say *play* in English, it's generally *spielen*.

Aussehen und Persönlichkeit – Appearance and Personality

Aussehen (n)	Appearance
dick	fat
dunkelhäutig	dark-skinned
fettleibig	obese
gebräunt	tanned
groß	tall
gut aussehend	good-looking
Haare (n pl)	hair
hässlich	ugly
Haut (f)	skin
hellhäutig	light-skinned
hübsch	pretty
kastanienbraun	chestnut
klein	short , small
lang	long
Rotschopf (m)	redhead
schlank	slim , slender
schön	beautiful
Sommersprosse (f)	freckle
stark	strong

Persönlichkeit (f)	Personality
egoistisch	selfish
faul	lazy
frech	cheeky
freundlich	friendly, pleasant
gemein	mean
lustig	funny
schüchtern	shy
stolz	proud

Wetter und Jahreszeiten – Weather and Seasons

Wetter (n)	Weather
bewölkt	cloudy
Blitz (m)	lightning
es regnet	it is raining
es schneit	it is snowing
Gewitter (n)	storm
Grad (m)	degree (temperature)
Himmel (m)	sky
kalt	cold
neblig	foggy
Regen (m)	rain
regnerisch	rainy
schlechtes Wetter	bad weather
Schnee (m)	snow
schön	good weather
Sonne (f)	sun
trocken	dry
Wärme (f)	heat
Wetterbericht (m)	weather report
Wind (m)	wind
windig	windy
Wolke (f)	cloud

Note: Talking about the weather is fairly easy in German (*it is sunny – es ist sonnig*), but don't forget that *it is snowing* is *es schneit* not *es ist schneit* (ouch!). See pg. 90 if you are unsure about the present tense. Also, note that you should use the simple past for weather in the past, rather than the perfect. So, don't say: *es ist bewölkt gewesen*; instead say: *es war bewölkt*.

Jahreszeiten (f pl)	Seasons
(im) Frühling (m)	(in) spring
(im) Sommer (m)	(in) summer
(im) Herbst (m)	(in) autumn
(im) Winter (m)	(in) winter

Kleidung und Mode – Clothes and Fashion

Kleidung (f)	Clothes
Anzug (m)	suit
Armbanduhr (f)	watch
Badeanzug (m)	swimming costume
Gürtel (m)	belt
Handschuh (m)	glove
Handtasche (f)	handbag
Hemd (n)	shirt
Hose (f) (**sg NOT pl**)	trousers
Hut (m)	hat
Krawatte (f)	tie
Mantel (m)	coat
Portemonnaie (n)	purse
Pullover (m)	sweater , jumper
Regenschirm (m)	umbrella
Rock (m)	skirt
Schal (m)	scarf
Schuh (m)	shoe
Socke (f)	sock
Trainingsanzug (m)	tracksuit
T-Shirt (n)	T-shirt
Turnschuhe (m pl)	trainers

Mode (f)	Fashion
aus Baumwolle	made of cotton
aus Leder	made of leather
aus Seide	made of silk
aus Wolle	made of wool
gestreift	stripy
getupft	spotted

Fächer – Subjects

Biologie (f)	biology
Chemie (f)	chemistry
Deutsch (n)	German
Englisch (n)	English
Erdkunde (f)	geography
Französisch (n)	French
Fremdsprachen (f pl)	foreign languages
Geschichte (f)	history
Informationstechnologie (f)	ICT
Kunst (f)	art
Mathe (f)	maths
Physik (f)	physics
Religion (f)	religious studies
Schauspielkunst (f)	drama , acting
Spanisch (n)	Spanish
Sport (m)	PE
Technik (f)	DT
Naturwissenschaften (f pl)	science , natural sciences

Transport – Transport

(mit dem) Flugzeug (n)	(by) plane
(mit dem) Motorrad (n)	(by) motorbike
(mit dem) Schiff (n)	(by) boat
(mit dem) Zug (m)	(by) train
fahren	to drive
Fahrschein (m)	ticket (for public transport)
Flugschein (m)	ticket (for a plane)
Verkehrsstau (m)	traffic jam
zu Fuß	on foot

Essen – Food (Difficult ones only!)

Obst (n sg)	Fruit
Ananas (f)	pineapple
Birne (f)	pear
Erdbeere (f)	strawberry
Himbeere (f)	raspberry
Kirsche (f)	cherry
Pampelmuse (f)	grapefruit
Pfirsich (m)	peach
Pflaume (f)	plum
Weintraube (f)	grape
Zitrone (f)	lemon

Gemüse (n sg)	Vegetables
Blumenkohl (m)	cauliflower
Erbsen (f pl)	peas
grüne Bohnen (f pl)	green beans
Gurke (f)	cucumber
Kartoffel (f)	potato
Kohl (m)	cabbage

im Allgemeinen	Generally
Ei (n)	egg
Eis (n)	ice cream
Fisch (m)	fish
Fleisch (n)	meat
Hähnchen (n)	chicken
Meeresfrüchte (f)	seafood
Pasta (f)	pasta
Pommes frites (f pl)	chips
Schinken (m)	ham
Suppe (f)	soup

Berufe – Professions

Arzt (m) / Ärztin (f)	doctor
Bäcker (m) / Bäckerin (f)	baker
Briefträger (m) / Briefträgerin (f)	postman / postwoman
Fahrer (m) / Fahrerin (f)	driver
Friseur (m) / Friseuse (f)	hairdresser
Hausmann (m) / Hausfrau (f)	house husband / house wife
Ingenieur (m) / Ingenieurin (f)	engineer
Kellner (m) / Kellnerin (f)	waiter / waitress
Krankenpfleger (m) / Krankenschwester (f)	nurse
Landwirt (m) / Landwirtin (f)	farmer
Lehrer (m) / Lehrerin (f)	teacher
Metzger (m) , Fleischer (m)	butcher
Polizist (m) / Polizistin (f)	police officer
Sekretär (m) / Sekretärin (f)	secretary
Soldat (m) / Soldatin (f)	soldier
Tierarzt (m) / Tierärztin (f)	vet
Verkäufer (m) / Verkäuferin (f)	shop assistant

Note: In German, you do **NOT** use an article (*einen, eine, ein,* etc.) before the name of a job. For example:

- *Meine Mutter ist Friseuse. – My mum is a hairdresser.*
- *Ich werde in der Zukunft Arzt sein. – I will be a doctor in the future.*

Die Umwelt – The Environment

Baum (m)	tree
erhöhen	to increase, to raise [something] (transitive)
sich verbessern	to improve
steigen	to increase (intransitive)

Note: An intransitive verb (e.g. *I go*) has no accusative direct object. You can't say *I go the car*. A transitive verb does have an object like that. For example, you can say *I wash the car*, because *to wash* is a transitive verb.

Abfall (m)	waste , trash
Abgase (n pl) , Auspuffgase (n pl)	exhaust fumes
Abholzung (f)	deforestation
Bereich (m)	area
Blechdose (f)	tin (can)
Brand (m)	fire
Eimer (m)	bin
Feld (n)	field
Glasflasche (f)	glass bottle
Grünfläche (f)	green space
Karton (m)	cardboard
laut	loud , noisy
Naturschutzgebiet	nature reserve
öffentliche Verkehrsmittel (n pl)	public transport
Plastiktüte (f)	plastic bag
Radweg (m)	cycle lane
reinigen	to clean , to purify
retten	to save
sauber	clean
schmutzig	dirty

Treibhauseffekt (m)	greenhouse effect
Verkehr (m)	traffic
Verpackung (f)	packaging
verschmutzt	polluted
verschwenden	to waste
Verschwendung (f)	waste , wastage
züchten	to grow

Little Annoying Words

The following words, no matter how little or annoying, are used very frequently and are important. So, if you don't know them, learn them! (We're expecting you to get déjà vu with most of these, as they crop up in lots of different places!)

allein	alone
allerdings	however
alles	everything
am besten	best of all
am meisten	most of all
am wenigsten	least of all
anders	different
auch	also
außerdem	moreover
beide	both
dagegen	on the other hand
deshalb	therefore
doch	but (used as a contradiction)
einschließlich	including
endlich	finally
erst	not until
fast	almost
früh	early
ganz	completely, whole

genau	exactly
gerade	just
gewöhnlich	usually
immer	always
in Ordnung	OK
insbesondere	especially
jemand	someone
jetzt	now
kaum	scarcely
keine Ahnung	no idea
keine Lust	no desire
leicht	simple, easy
leider	unfortunately
manchmal	sometimes
mehr als	more than
mindestens	at least
nachher	afterwards
noch	still
noch etwas	in addition , something else
nur	only
plötzlich	suddenly
schon	already
selten	seldom
sofort	straight away
sogar	even
sondern	but rather
sonst	otherwise
spät	late
stimmt	that's right , correct
überall	everywhere
ungefähr	about
unmöglich	impossible

verboten	banned
viel	much, a lot
vielleicht	perhaps
von Zeit zu Zeit	from time to time
vor allem	above all
vorher	beforehand
wahrscheinlich	probably
wenig	few, little
wieder	again
wirklich wichtig	really important
zu (laut)	too (loud)
zufällig	by chance
zum Glück	luckily
zurück	back

Negatives

As we're looking at little, annoying words, you may want visit pg. 55, where there is a list of ones which negate a sentence. There are also a couple of Golden Nuggets about these on pg. 140.

Falsche Freunde

These German words are similar to words in English, but actually mean something entirely different from their lookalikes. **Examiners love these!**

aktuell	current
also	thus , therefore
Art (f)	type , kind
Bad (n)	bath
bald	soon
bekommen	to get
Billion (f)	trillion

Chef (m)	boss, head of the dept.
eventuell	maybe , possibly
Fabrik (f)	factory
fast	almost
Fotograf (m)	photographer
Gift (n)	poison
Gymnasium (n)	secondary school
Handy (n)	mobile phone
Hochschule (f)	college , university
Kritik (f)	criticism
Mist (m)	dung , manure
Mörder (m)	murderer
Noten (f pl)	marks , grades (at school)
Publikum (n)	audience
Rat (m)	advice
realisieren	to implement , to carry out , to produce (a film)
Rente (f)	pension
Rezept (n)	recipe
Roman (m)	novel
Smoking (m)	tuxedo , dinner jacket
Spot (m)	advert (on TV)
sympathisch	likable , nice
tasten	to touch
Tipp (m)	hint
Unternehmer (m)	business person , employer
Wand (f)	wall

Cutting Out Grammar Errors
....

When you write in German, you need to turn yourself into a computer which follows a series of steps to produce a word-by-word, grammatically correct sentence. Do this over and over again and you will have a number of grammatically correct sentences which form a grammatically correct essay. Simple.

The biggest hindrance to this is forgetfulness. Because we are all used to talking in English without thinking about grammar, we naturally write in German in a similar way. You translate words from English to German in your head, and then write them down to form sentences. We have to override this natural flow of words to make our minds focus on the grammar involved. We must concentrate on each word to ensure we do not forget to make things grammatically correct. The sections which follow aim to give you the ability to cut out grammar errors... You just have to make sure you remember to follow the rules.

> **GOLDEN RULE :**
> **DON'T FORGET GRAMMAR**

Ohhh... and one more thing you have heard a couple of times before:

> **GOLDEN RULE :**
> **WRITE WHAT YOU KNOW, DON'T WRITE WHAT YOU**
> **DON'T KNOW**

Verbs

When studying languages, all students tend to hate verbs! They are the most important part of any language in order to boost your grade grammatically because the simple fact is: knowing how to use verbs instantly makes you stand out as a strong candidate. In reality, they are very straightforward. You merely need to know:

- Which tense to use
- How to form each tense according to:
    - Which tense you are using
    - Which person you are using from:

Person	German	English	Example
1st Person Singular	ich	I	I need some money.
2nd Person Singular	du	you (singular familiar)	You eat too much.
3rd Person Singular	er or sie es man 'a noun'	he or she or it it you (in general) 'a noun'	Monty released the hounds.
1st Person Plural	wir '1 or more nouns' und ich	we '1 or more nouns' and I	Susie and I like to eat spinach.
2nd Person Plural	ihr	you (plural familiar)	You two should not have done that.
3rd Person Plural	sie '2 or more nouns'	they '2 or more nouns'	Tim, John and Richard have no friends.
2nd Person Polite	Sie	you (polite form, singular & plural)	You didn't set us any homework!

We are now going to take you through what each tense means and when each tense should be used. Then we shall look - precisely and in a very easy-to-understand way - at how you can ensure you don't make any grammar errors using each tense, and therefore boost your grade.

What each tense means

First of all, let's look at what each tense is used for in German along with examples (in English) of when it would be used. First, the indicative or 'normal' tenses:

Tenses	To...
Present	1) Say what you **normally** do.
	2) Say what you are **currently** doing.
	3) Say what will happen in the **near future**.
	E.g.1 I *play in the park all the time.*
	E.g.2 I *am eating a sausage.*
	E.g.3 I *am going to his party on Saturday.*
Simple Past	1) Say what happened (i.e. some kind of completed action in the past.)
	2) Give a general description in the past (normally of an opinion).
	3) Describe what you **used** to do.
	4) Describe a continuing state in the past, including something that **was** happening **when** suddenly something else happened.
	E.g.1 I *saw my mates and then* **spoke** *to them.*
	E.g.2 *The firework display* **was** *thrilling.*
	E.g.3 I *used to sail all the time.*
	E.g.4 I **was** *doing my homework* **when** *my dad came in.*

Perfect	1. Describe a completed action in the past.
	2. Say *I **have** never / always + past participle…*
	3. Describe something that has happened but is still relevant to the present.
	E.g.1 *I **passed** my German exam.*
	E.g.2 *I **have** always thought of going to the Brazil, but I **have** never really liked hot weather.*
	E.g.3 *It **has been** snowing today.*

Note: Don't forget that if you're using *seit* to say something like *I have been learning Portuguese since March,* you must use the present tense in German, not a past tense. The logic is that you are still learning Portuguese, so it's a present action.

Pluperfect	Often describe something longer ago in the past than the perfect tense. It is used whenever in English you say *I **had** + past participle.*
	E.g. *Once I **had** asked my mum for permission, I went to my friend's house.*
Future	1. Say what you **will** do in the more distant future.
	2. Say what you will do in the near future, if the present tense doesn't make it clear that you're talking about something that is yet to happen.
	E.g.1 *I **will** see Japan when I leave school.*
	E.g.2 ***I'm coming round.***

Future Perfect	1. Say what you **will**, or hope to, **have** done in the future when (by the time) something else happens.
	2. Say what you suppose has happened.
	E.g.1 *I **will have** finished my work by the time the bell goes.*
	E.g.2 *Henry **will have** left work by now.*

Note: As you may be aware, there isn't a 'conditional tense' (like you would find in other European languages) as such. Instead, there's Subjunctive II - the second type of the subjunctive.

Lots of info about this on pg. 93.

Despite the lack of a conditional tense, the subjunctive is pretty handy to express a conditional: *If I had a lot of money, I **would**...* One more thing: like the indicative above, subjunctive II does have different 'tenses' or different forms, but we're going to keep things relatively simple...!

Now, the types of subjunctive II:

'Present', like our normal/indicative 'Conditional'	1. Portray something theoretical. It is used in English whenever you say *I **would**...*
	2. Be polite when stating, asking or requesting.
	E.g.1 *I **would** try skydiving, if I had the courage.*
	E.g.2 *That's all.* (Das **wäre** alles.) or
	I would like... (Ich **möchte**...)
'Past', like our normal/indicative 'Conditional Perfect'	Portray something theoretical in the past. It is used in English whenever you say *I **would have** + past participle.*
	E.g. *I **would have** gone to the party, if I had found the time.*

Getting Rid of Verb Errors

The tables we have just seen are probably fairly scary ones. There are 8 tenses included... "That is all far too difficult when you can barely work out how to use the present tense" is what many school teachers would tell you. This is a load of rubbish! In fact, the present and simple past tenses are by far the hardest of the tenses to use and form, and if you have even the slightest grasp of these, using the other tenses really is easier. Trust us; the supposedly more difficult and complex tenses towards the end of the previous table, which will gain you **LOADS OF MARKS,** really are simple to form.

So, let's go through each tense and work out how to boost your grammar mark by using each correctly.

> **Note:** Unlike other languages, there isn't so much distinction between the uses of the perfect tense and the simple past tense in German. Generally, the simple past is used more in writing than in conversation, but you'll still use the simple past forms of *haben (hatte), sein (war), werden (wurde)* and the modals *(musste, konnte, wollte,* and so on) when you're speaking. In your essay(s) at (I)GCSE level, you should be fine with the perfect for most verbs, but do use these verbs in the simple past, where appropriate.

Weak, Strong, Regular, Irregular

The following terminology is used frequently in this section, so here is a little guide.

Weak verbs are the easy ones like *machen*, which are completely 'regular'. The stem of a weak verb stays the same in every part of each of the indicative (or 'normal') tenses.

Strong verbs are ones like *sprechen*, which involve a vowel change in the stem. (An English example of this is *to drink... drink, drank, drunk.*) Any change can normally be seen in the simple past, but you will also find some alterations in the present and the perfect. Strong verbs can be considered 'irregular' because of this complexity.

So, how do we form the **stem**? As a general rule, take the infinitive (e.g. *spielen*) and remove the '-en' (e.g. *spiel*) or just the '-n' (e.g. *ändern* becomes *änder*). For weak verbs, this is the building block of all the indication tenses, from the present to the future perfect! Be careful with strong verbs, though, because things are not that simple, as can be seen in the rest of this section. It is worth noting that lots of common, everyday verbs are strong verbs, so there's no escaping them! Have a look at pg. 56 for how stems change across the tenses.

Finally, there are those '**fully irregulars**' (e.g. *sein*), which look different all over the place (e.g. *bin, sind, war, gewesen*), but luckily for us, there aren't many of them to learn!

Present Tense

As we have said, the present tense is often difficult, because you have to be aware of the different ways strong verbs behave. For example, *I see* is *ich sehe* in German, but *he sees* is *er sieht*. (Notice the sudden appearance of a vowel.) Changes like this just have to be learnt, but don't try to memorise the behaviour of every single strong verb in every tense; that is pretty unrealistic and actually unnecessary to achieve a top grade. What you should do first, though, is look at pg. 56 and make sure you know how to form every verb on that page in the different tenses. Also, don't forget about the infinitive: it is crucial.

Now, simply, to form the present tense, take the stem and add the endings in the table below, according to the subject/person of the verb (see pg. 85). This is the same for both weak and strong verbs.

Pronoun	Ending
ich	-e
du	-(e)st
er/sie/es	-(e)t
wir	-en
ihr	-t
sie/Sie	-en

There are, of course, a couple of added complications… Where the stem ends in '-chn', '-d', '-dn' or '-t', you need to put in an extra 'e' (shown in brackets in the table) for pronunciation purposes. This is similar to the 'stutter verbs' rule on the next page. Also, where the stem ends in '-s', '-ß', '-ss' or '-z', the ending for the *du* form is just '-t', to avoid ridiculous things like *du issst*! (*You eat* is just *du isst*.)

Be aware that you will need to know *haben, sein* and *werden* inside out, because of their uses in multiple 'compound' tenses like the perfect and the future.

There are two golden saviours for when you are not certain of a verb's formation. The first saviour is using a phrase (see pg. 37 onwards), many of which simply require you to know the infinitive of the verb you want to use. The second saviour is verbs that take an infinitive: '**modal verbs**'. The best ones to use are:

	können (to be able to)	**müssen** (to have to)	**wollen** (to want to)	**sollen** (to be supposed to)
ich	kann	muss	will	soll
du	kannst	musst	willst	sollst
er/sie/es	kann	muss	will	soll
wir	können	müssen	wollen	sollen
ihr	könnt	müsst	wollt	sollt
sie/Sie	können	müssen	wollen	sollen

So, if we wanted to say: *she eats an apple every day,* but couldn't remember the parts of *essen* (which we should know!), we could change the sentence slightly:

*Sie **isst** einen Apfel jeden Tag.* – She **eats** an apple every day.
*Sie **muss** jeden Tag einen Apfel essen.* – She **has** to eat an apple every day.

Note: There is lots of help about word order with modals on pg. 133.

Simple Past Tense

The simple past (a.k.a. the 'preterite' or the 'imperfect') is only really called 'simple' because it's got one bit, rather than an auxiliary verb (*haben* or *sein*) and a past participle like the perfect. The hard bit is knowing how strong verbs change from what they look like in the present (e.g. *fahren* becomes *ich fuhr*). These verbs use the strong endings below and must be learnt so that you are be able to recognise them. For weak verbs, like *machen*, take the infinitive, remove the '-en' (or '-n' e.g. *ändern*) to form the stem and add the weak endings. However, probably the only verbs you will need to use in the simple past are the modals, which are hardly ever used in the perfect tense, along with *haben, sein* and *werden,* of course.

Pronoun	Weak	Strong
ich	-te	-
du	-test	-st
er/sie/es	-te	-
wir	-ten	-en
ihr	-tet	-t
sie/Sie	-ten	-en

Note: There is a group of verbs that we call 'stutter verbs'. Generally when the stem ends in '-chn', '-d', '-dn' or '-t', we add an extra 'e' before the endings above to make the simple past (more) pronounceable. E.g. *arbeiten* becomes *ich arbeitete* and *regnen* becomes *es regnete.*

Also, be aware that some verbs act like strong verbs and have letter changes, but then use the weak endings (e.g. *denken* becomes *ich dachte*).

In proper written German, the simple past is used more than the perfect, but as we've said before, at (I)GCSE you can get a good grade using the perfect tense in your essays for most things in the past. However - to prove to the examiner that you know what it looks like and how to use it - use the simple past with modals, *haben, sein, werden* and particularly for phrases such as:

1. *das war* (from *sein*) meaning *it / that was* along with an adjective to demonstrate your opinion of something.
2. Use *es gab* (from *geben*) meaning *there was* or *there were*. (For more on *es gibt* constructions have a look at pg. 143.)
3. Describe the weather in the past using *es war...* E.g. *Es war sonnig, und wir sind deshalb in den Garten gegangen.*

Having said all of that, don't write your essays all in the simple past, because you won't be able to show off your knowledge of how to form the perfect and of which verbs take *haben* and which verbs take *sein* in the perfect! (See pg. 98.)

Future & 'Conditional' Tenses – The Subjunctive in German

The future tense is the easiest of any tense in German, as long as you know *werden!* All you have to do is take the relevant subject (*ich, du, sie*, etc.) and the corresponding bit of *werden* in the **present** tense, and then put the infinitive of the verb you want at the end of the clause:

Subject	Werden	...	Infinitive	English
Ich	werde	(im Hotel)	sein	I will be (in the hotel)
Sie	wird	(das Geld)	haben	She will have (the money)
Sie	werden	(Orangensaft)	trinken	They will drink orange juice

Note: Below is some complex linguistic stuff. Try to understand as much as you can, because it'll help!

In German, there is no conditional tense like there is in other European languages. However, there is a way of translating *I would go to the party, if I had enough time* and it's by using the subjunctive. The subjunctive is what nerds like us call a 'mood'. Verbs as you know them are normally 'indicative' (*I go, they spoke, you will see*), and that's another mood. The subjunctive is generally about doubt and it's even used in English in this way! *"If I were you, I'd..."* (*"...but I'm not you, so how would I know?!"*) (Of course, most people say *"If I was you"* nowadays, which is technically wrong, but who really cares?)

In German, there are two types of subjunctive. The good news is that **you only have to worry about the second type**, shown in this book as *Subjunctive II*. (If you're interested, the first type is for reported speech, but you'll learn all about that next year!)

Now: the really important bit… The easiest way of dealing with subjunctive II is to use the right form of *werden* - basically just the simple past with an umlaut (two dots) on the u (ü) - and an infinitive:

Subject	Würden	…	Infinitive	English
Du	würdest	(in die Stadt)	gehen	You (sg) would go (into town)
Er	würde	(den Mann)	sehen	He would see (the man)
Sie	würden	(mein Auto)	waschen	They would wash my car

With the future tense, it may be helpful to think of the *werden* bit as the *will* bit in English (e.g. *I **will** go*), and then with the subjunctive the *werden* changes to *würden* just as the *will* bit changes to *would* (e.g. *I **would** go*).

If you're thinking that the examples in the table don't really make sense, we agree with you! This use of subjunctive II has a condition, whether stated or implied (in context): *I would go to the club, **if** my parents allowed it.*

As with most of these things, *haben, sein, werden* (as you've just seen) and the modals are a bit different, because Germans don't use the method above with them! Luckily, though, for each of these (except wollen and sollen) all you have to do is add an umlaut to the simple past form:

Ich hatte → ich hätte	wir konnten → wir könnten
du warst → du wärst	ihr wollt → ihr wollt
er wurde → er würde	sie sollen → sie sollten

Note: So, how do we say *I **would go** to the party, if I **had** enough time*?

*Ich **würde** auf die Party **gehen**, wenn ich genug Zeit **hätte**.*

Notice how we can tell that the party's either still going on or will happen in the future. Let's suppose you missed that awesome night out. See pg. 98-99 for how to say *I would have gone to the party, if I had been invited.*

Perfect, Pluperfect & Future Perfect

Now we are coming towards what are generally considered the 'very difficult' and 'advanced' tenses. However, these three tenses are all formed in a very similar way. Rather than having a pronoun or a noun and one other word, these have a pronoun or a noun and at least two other words:

Pronoun or **Noun** + **Part of** *haben* or **Part of** *sein* + **Past Participle**

E.g.　　　　**Georg**　　　　　　　　**hat**　　　　　　　　**gegessen**

To form these three compound tenses, you simply need to use a different tense of *haben* or *sein* (and we have already covered each of these three tenses)! So, which tense of *haben* or *sein* do you need to use for each compound tense?

Compound Tense	Tense of *haben* or *sein*
Perfect	Present
Pluperfect	Simple Past
Future Perfect	Future

Note: So which is it… *haben* or *sein*? Don't panic! This is covered on pg. 98.

Therefore, the three most important verbs for you to succeed in German are *haben, sein* and *werden*. You need to know **all six parts** of **all** of them in the **present**, **simple past** and **future** like you know how to spell your name (hopefully!). These are so important.

> **GOLDEN RULE :**
> **LEARN *HABEN, SEIN & WERDEN***

haben – to have

	Present	Simple Past	Future
ich	habe	hatte	werde…haben
du	hast	hattest	wirst…haben
er/sie/es	hat	hatte	wird…haben
wir	haben	hatten	werden…haben
ihr	habt	hattet	werdet…haben
sie/Sie	haben	hatten	werden…haben

Past participle – *gehabt*
Auxiliary verb – *haben* (*Ich habe gehabt*)

sein – to be

	Present	Simple Past	Future
ich	bin	war	werde…sein
du	bist	warst	wirst…sein
er/sie/es	ist	war	wird…sein
wir	sind	waren	werden…sein
ihr	seid	wart	werdet…sein
sie/Sie	sind	waren	werden…sein

Past participle – *gewesen*
Auxiliary verb – *sein* (*Ich bin gewesen*)

So, now we have the pronoun or noun and the part of *haben* or part of *sein* sorted, what about the past participle? Back on pg. 95, we saw the example: *Georg hat gegessen.* If we look at this sentence grammatically, *gegessen* is a past participle. In English, most past participles end in *-ed* or *-en*. E.g. played (*gespielt*), driven (*gefahren*), eaten (*gegessen*), spoken (gesprochen). In German, you have to watch out for vowel changes, like that last one: *sprechen* becomes *gesprochen*. Fortunately for you, past participles are used in German in pretty much the same way as in English. Slightly less fortunately, there are quite a few odd-looking ones that you need to learn (e.g. *gehen* becomes *gegangen*)!

How to form a Past Participle

For the weak verbs in German, the past participle is formed in the following way:

Infinitive	Remove	On the left add	On the right add	Past participle
machen	-en	ge-	-t	*gemacht*
sagen	-en	ge-	-t	*gesagt*

For strong verbs, learning is required, as these verbs have vowel changes and sometimes consonant changes too. However, there are patterns to follow, which make things a lot easier. (See pg. 56, and compare *nehmen, schwimmen* and *sprechen*, for example.) For now, though:

Infinitive	Remove	On the left add	Fun stuff	On the right add	Past participle
gehen	-en	ge-	eh → ang	-en	*gegangen*
bringen	-en	ge-	ing → ach	-t	*gebracht*
fließen	-en	ge-	ieß → oss	-en	*geflossen*

It's worth removing the '-en' in your head, even if you're going to add it later, as you get used to making the 'stem', which is useful for things like the present tense.

'Conditional Perfect' – More Subjunctive in German

Just as with the 'conditional', which we saw a few pages ago, what might be called the 'conditional perfect' tense in other European languages doesn't exist in German. However, using subjunctive II, we can get pretty much the same thing.

Pronoun or Noun + Subj II of *haben* or Subj II of *sein* + Past Participle

You'll see some examples of this kind of thing in just a moment, but essentially this is for when you want to say what you would have done, if the chance had arisen, or what would have happened under a set of circumstances that did not come to pass.

Haben or *Sein*?

In German, as we have just seen, the perfect, pluperfect and future perfect are formed by using the right tense of *haben* or *sein*, or the subjunctive II form of the same verbs for the 'conditional perfect'. With either type, you also need the right past participle. Now, the dilemma: which do you use? *Haben* or *sein*?

Note that when we say 'take *sein*', this means that whenever any of the above tenses or constructions is used, the part that goes with the pronoun (*ich, du*, etc.) must be a part of *sein* (never *haben*) (e.g. **er ist**... *gegangen*).

Most verbs in German take *haben* in these tenses. The verbs that take sein are intransitive.

Woah! Hang on a moment! What is this 'intranstive' of which you speak?

Linguistically, intransitive verbs do not have a direct object in the accusative case. To rephrase that, most of these verbs can't be followed by 'a thing' and still make sense. *Gehen* and *vorkommen* are intranstive and you can't *go a thing* or *occur a thing*. On the other hand, *machen* and *schlagen* are transitive - you can quite happily 'do / make a thing' or 'hit a thing'.

> **Note:** This does not always work, though, so it's better to understand what a direct object in the accusative case is. For this, see pg. 119. E.g. *folgen – to follow*. You can *follow a thing*, but it's *Ich **bin** ihr gefolgt – I have followed her*. This is the same for *bleiben* and *sein* itself (*stay / be a thing*).

Another way to think about this is the idea of a change of state. E.g. *the light went out – das Licht **ist** ausgegangen*. E.g.2 *the snow had already melted – der Schnee **war** schon geschmolzen*.

As in the note above, *bleiben* and *sein* both take *sein*! This is just a reminder that you use them with the nominative case, because you're dealing with the same person or thing. E.g. *he is a man – er ist ein Mann*. *'Ein Mann'* is nominative, because both the 'he' and 'the man' are the same person. If it's nominative, it's not accusative! Therefore, it takes *sein*.

Examples of the Perfect, Pluperfect, Future Perfect & 'Conditional Perfect'

Just to give you an idea of how you might use these tenses in an essay, here are some sample sentences.

> **Note:** There are also some phrases starting on pg. 37 containing these tenses, but we're hoping that, once you understand the grammar, you will be able to make your own ones up too.

Perfect: **Ich habe** immer Fußball **gespielt**, weil **ich** immer viele Tore **geschossen habe**. – **I have** always **played** football, because **I've** always **scored** many goals.

Pluperfect: Natürlich wollte ich nach Hause fahren! **Ich hatte** so viele Pommes **gegessen**, dass **ich** im Restaurant krank **geworden war**. – Of course I wanted to go home! **I had eaten** so many chips that **I had fallen** ill in the restaurant.

Future Perfect: Um 23 Uhr **werde ich** meine Hausaufgaben **gemacht haben**! – At eleven o'clock **I will have done** my homework!

Conditional Perfect: Wenn **ich** genug Geld **verdient hätte**, **wäre ich** nach Amerika **geflogen**. – If **I had earnt** enough money, **I would have flown** to America.

And another conditional perfect, as promised on pg. 94: **Ich wäre** auf die Party **gegangen**, wenn **ich** eingeladen **worden wäre**. – **I would have gone** to the party, if **I had been** invited. This one involves a passive (see pg. 103) as well as the subjunctive, and is therefore far beyond what you are expected to know. Only consider using this type of phrase once you are confident with the simpler ones.

Reflexives

So what are reflexive verbs? They are verbs which involve someone doing something to himself / herself. So, for example, in German *ich setze mich* translates literally to *I sit myself down*. There are quite a few reflexive verbs and they are mostly for describing your daily routine or your injuries. They behave in the same way as ordinary verbs, except that you have to add in an extra 'part' when you form reflexive verbs. These parts need to agree with the pronoun / noun.

Pronoun or **Noun + Main Part of Verb + Extra Part = Fully Formed Reflexive**

So what is this extra part? Well, it depends. Sometimes it's just an accusative, other times it's a dative. Taking *sich waschen* as an example, *Ich wasche mich* is just I wash (myself). However, if you say that you're washing your hands, your hands are now the direct object (see pg. 119) and so the reflexive 'extra part' becomes dative: *Ich wasche mir die Hände – I wash to myself the hands*!

Note: The tables for the 'extra part', or the 'reflexive pronoun', in both the accusative and the dative, can be found on pg. 126, in the pronouns section.

Reflexives have lots of variations and rules, which aren't important at this stage. Just remember that reflexives in one of those compound tenses (perfect, pluperfect, future perfect or 'conditional perfect') take *haben*.

Separable Verbs

These are verbs with prefixes which separate from the rest of the verb in multiple forms. Separable verbs include *aufstehen* (*to stand / get up*) and *zumachen* (*to close*). Let's see how they work.

There are plenty of prefixes to get used to. They all work in exactly the same way, but if you know what they mean, they might help you out in a reading comprehension if you come across a new separable verb.

ab-, an-, auf-, aus-, ein-, her-, hin-, mit-, nach-, vor-, vorbei-, weg-, weiter-, zu-, zurück-, zusammen-

Some of these look like prepositions (which we'll cover on pg. 121), others like adverbs. So, if you know that *ein-* is comparable to the English prefix 'in-', then you'll know that *einkommen* means 'to come in' or 'to enter'. Similarly, you might not immediately recognise a verb, but if you see *zurück-*, chances are it'll be about going back or returning to a previous state.

Hopefully, the following table will demonstrate what happens with a separable verb. We're using *aufstehen* which is a *sein* verb (see pg. 98), but there are also separable verbs which take *haben*.

Verb	Tense / Type	Sentence
	Present	Ich **stehe** um sieben Uhr **auf**
	Simple Past	Ich **stand** um sieben Uhr **auf**.
	Perfect	Ich bin um sieben Uhr **aufgestanden**.
	Future	Ich werde um sieben Uhr **aufstehen**.
aufstehen	Modals	Ich will um sieben Uhr **aufstehen**.
	zu	Ich hoffe, um sieben Uhr **aufzustehen**.
	weil	..., weil ich um sieben Uhr **aufstehe**.
	Imperatives	**Stehen** Sie **auf**! **Steh auf**!
	Questions	**Stehen** Sie **auf**? **Stehst** du **auf**?

So, the main points:

You quite often see the separable prefix at the end of the clause / sentence on its own, but certain tenses and phrases change that. The past participle of separable verbs has the '-ge-' bit between the prefix and the normal verb part. The infinitive (for use with the future tense and modals, for example) is also one word, as is what you get in a *zu* clause: the *zu*, like the '-ge-' bit goes in the middle. In subordinate clauses (like you get with *weil, obwohl, als,* etc.) the verb goes as one word at the end of the clause. But what happens if we combine two of those sentence types?

…because I got up at 07:00. – …, weil ich um sieben Uhr aufgestanden bin.

This is just like any other normal verb - the finite verb (*'bin'*, this time) goes right at the end, with the past participle just before.

Don't worry too much about the different types of word order - there's a whole section on it (from pg. 130)! Just accept that separable verbs aren't that different to normal verbs, once you know to put the '-ge-' in the middle of the past participle (see pg. 97 on how to form this) and the *zu* in the middle of the infinitive:

Verb (Infinitive)	Past Participle	With *zu*
ablehnen	**ab**gelehnt	**ab**zulehnen
ankommen	**an**gekommen	**an**zukommen
aufgeben	**auf**gegeben	**auf**zugeben
ausgehen	**aus**gegangen	**aus**zugehen

As you can see, the past participles are just like they would be normally, only with a prefix. *gehen* → *gegangen, ausgehen* → *ausgegangen.*

Another example:

Obwohl ich **ausgehen** *sollte, weil ich meine Freundin* **angerufen** *hatte, war ich nicht in der Lage, mich* **aufzumachen**. *Ich ging in mein Zimmer, und dann* **schlief** *ich* **ein**. – Although I was supposed to go out, because my girlfriend had rung, I was unable to sally forth. I went into my bedroom and then fell asleep.

Separable verbs aren't essential, but you will have to recognise them and they're fairly useful. And it's a way of testing your grammar!

The Passive Voice

There is one more distinction to be made before we move away from verbs for a bit. Most sentences are 'active' or 'in the active voice'.

The boy <mark>threw</mark> the stone.

We've got our subject, our <mark>verb</mark> and our object. This sentence is active (not because the boy is being athletic or anything like that), because the subject, 'the boy', is doing the action stated by the verb. A passive sentence is different:

The stone <mark>was thrown</mark> by the boy.

Now, 'the stone' is the subject, but it has not been doing anything itself; it was <u>being</u> thrown. This is a 'passive' sentence, or a sentence 'in the passive voice'. Technically, the accusative object of the active sentence has become the subject of the passive sentence. Also, notice how we haven't highlighted 'the boy' in blue in the second sentence. This is because 'the boy' is not an object, but an 'agent' - the entity who is still doing something (throwing the stone), but is not the subject of the sentence. The agent is often left out in a passive sentence.

You won't *have to* use the passive yourself, but if you do, <u>you will impress</u>.

So, now we've got that sorted in English… In German, there are two different forms of the passive: one made with *werden*, the other with *sein*. The difference between the two can be hard to understand.

What they look like:

***werden*-passive**	Die Tür wurde zugesperrt.	The door was locked.
***sein*-passive**	Die Tür war zugesperrt.	The door was locked.

The following sentence was designed to help explain the difference: Als ich um sieben Uhr kam, **war** die Tür **zugesperrt**, aber ich weiß nicht, wann sie **zugesperrt wurde**. – When I came at seven, the door **was locked**, but I don't know when it **was locked**.

The passive with *werden*, then, is more about the action, the process (e.g. 'the door was becoming locked'), whereas the passive with *sein* is more about the state of things upon the completion of the action. We'll be focussing more on the *werden*-passive, because it's used much more frequently.

So how do we form the passive?

Simply, we take a noun or a pronoun in the nominative case (see pg. 119), add a suitable part of *werden* (or *sein*) and end with a past participle. If we want to specify who or what is responsible for the action, we can include the agent (using the prepositions *von* or *durch* to express 'by').

Subject	werden	Agent	Past Participle	English
Das Geld	wird	von dem Dieb	gestohlen.	The money is being stolen by the thief.

The sentence is set-up. All we have to do now is change the tense of *werden* as required.

Das Geld wurde gestohlen.	The money was stolen.
Das Geld ist gestohlen worden.	The money was / has been stolen.
Das Geld war gestohlen worden.	The money had been stolen.
Das Geld wird gestohlen werden.	The money will be stolen.
Das Geld wird gestohlen worden sein.	The money will have been stolen.
Das Geld würde gestohlen werden.	The money would be stolen.
Das Geld wäre gestohlen worden.	The money would have been stolen.

You will notice that the past participle we're using for *werden* itself is *worden*, not *geworden* as you might expect. This is mainly a stylistic thing for passive sentences, but it is actually considered wrong to use *geworden* here! (It's *geworden* when *werden* is used to mean 'to become' e.g. *er ist Arzt geworden*.)

Tip: Don't know *werden*? LEARN IT! It's so crucial for passives, yes, but also for indispensable things like the future tense! It's printed on the next page for your convenience.

Note: If you're desperate to say *the money could have been stolen*, watch out for confusing word order. You might want to brush up on it: see pg. 130.

That is pretty much it for the basics of the passive. If you can get just one passive sentence into your essay, even if it's in the present tense, you're proving to the examiner that you know how to form it and use it! Don't try to be over-adventurous, because it'll hurt you if you're wrong!

werden – to become

	Present	**Simple Past**	**Future**
ich	werde	wurde	werde…werden
du	wirst	wurdest	wirst…werden
er/sie/es	wird	wurde	wird…werden
wir	werden	wurden	werden…werden
ihr	werdet	wurdet	werdet…werden
sie/Sie	werden	wurden	werden…werden

Past participle – _geworden_ (_worden_ in passive sentences)
Auxiliary verb – _sein_ (_Ich bin geworden_)

To form the subjunctive II form of _werden_, just add umlauts to the 'u's of the simple past → _ich würde_

Articles & Adjectives

This section is so incredibly important, but don't fret; we've done our best to make it comprehensible!

Articles are the short words that go in front of the bigger words. In English, they're words like *a*, *an* and *the*. In German, they include *der, die, das, ein, eine* and all their 'changed forms' like *dem* and *einen*. They have to change depending on the noun they go with. Think of this change like *a* becoming *an* for English words beginning with a vowel. In German, though we're looking at our old friends: number, gender and case.

> **Note:** Number – whether the noun is singular or plural. Gender – whether the noun is masculine, feminine or neuter. Case – whether the noun is nominative, accusative, genitive or dative. See pg. 114 if you are unsure about any of this.

Adjectives are words which describe nouns. In German, unlike in English, there is the complication of agreements: if an adjective comes directly before the noun it describes, it also has to agree in number, case and gender. However, if it comes afterwards, there is no agreement at all! Agreements are crucial and must be mastered for a top grade.

For both articles and adjectives, 'to agree is to end'. You have to change the endings as the tables on the next page will show you.

Many students seem to panic when they hear that 'dreaded' word: agreements. However, this really is not too difficult... It is easier than what we have just covered in the *Verbs* section, because there are unambiguous rules to follow. Essentially, when you learn adjectives, they are given in its most basic form, without endings. You need to be comfortable with the process of changing that form.

The first table shows adjective endings with the **definite** article: *der, die, das*, etc. These endings are also used after *dieser, welcher, jeder, jener, mancher* and *alle*, and their variations (*dieses, diese*, etc.).

The second shows adjective endings with the **indefinite** article: *ein, eine, ein*, etc. The endings in the second table are also used after *mein, dein, sein, ihr, unser, Ihr* and *euer* - bascially, any word like that which shows possession - plus *kein*, which makes it negative: *Ich habe kein Buch – I don't have a book.*

In the tables below, the endings the adjectives are highlighted in yellow, and any endings to the noun are in blue. For these, the endings in the plural are the same for all three genders.

DEFINITE	Singular			Plural
	Masculine	Feminine	Neuter	
Nominative	der gute Mann	die nette Frau	das neue Buch	die alten Leute
Accusative	den guten Mann	die nette Frau	das neue Buch	die alten Leute
Genitive	des guten Mannes	der netten Frau	des neuen Buches	der alten Leute
Dative	dem guten Mann	der netten Frau	dem neuen Buch	den alten Leuten

As you can see, in the masculine, genitive singular and the neuter, genitive singular there's the extra ending of '-es'. For most single syllable nouns you should add this ending; for longer nouns it's normally just an '-s'. Also, there's an '-n' at the end of nouns in the dative plural. What we've also done is split the table up into two (look at the green shading). This shows that there are really only two adjective endings to know for the above table: '-e' and '-en'. That all changes with the indefinite table below!

INDEFINITE	Singular			Plural
	Masculine	Feminine	Neuter	
Nominative	ein guter Mann	eine nette Frau	ein neues Buch	keine alten Leute
Accusative	einen guten Mann	eine nette Frau	ein neues Buch	keine alten Leute
Genitive	eines guten Mannes	einer netten Frau	eines neuen Buches	keiner alten Leute
Dative	einem guten Mann	einer netten Frau	einem neuen Buch	keinen alten Leuten

As marked by the red shading, we've got a couple of new adjective endings in the masculine, nominative singular, and in the neuter, nominative singular and the neuter, accusative singular. The green shading shows again that lots of the endings are just '-en'! It may be helpful to remember that there's the shape of a pan in both tables where there's no green shading: a 'pan of -e' and a 'pan of mixture'! You'll also notice that we change 'eine' to 'keine' in the plural. This is because you can't say 'a wooden chairs' but you can say 'no wooden chairs'.

But what happens if we just want to say we drank good wine'? There's no article there! This is where the 'zero declension' steps in. What we've been doing is 'declining' adjectives - getting the right endings for the job. So, the 'zero declension' is the set of adjective endings when there is no *der, die, das, ein, eine, mein, meine* or any of that lot... but there are other words which use it - see below.

ZERO	Singular			Plural
	Masculine	Feminine	Neuter	
Nominative	guter Wein	dicke Sahne	frishes Brot	arme Leute
Accusative	guten Wein	dicke Sahne	frisches Brot	arme Leute
Genitive	guten Weins	dicker Sahne	frischen Brots	armer Leute
Dative	gutem Wein	dicker Sahne	frischem Brot	armen Leuten

Whilst this table can look daunting initially, consider the articles in the *der, die, das* table. With the exception of the ones shaded in red here, just think of the adjective as if it were the definite article: *guter Wein* looks remarkably like *der Wein*, the same goes for *dicke Sahne* and *die Sahne*, and *frisches Brot* and *das Brot*. (Just remember that it's not *frischas Brot* or *dickie Sahne*!) Also, note that, as we said earlier, the genitive ending '-s' is used here in the masculine and neuter singular, but this could quite happily be '-es' (*Weines, Brotes*) - play it by ear!

You also use the zero declension adjective endings following *ein paar* (a few), *einige* (some , a few), *manche* (some), *viele* (many), *mehrere* (several) and *wenige* (few). Note that 'a few' and 'few' are not the same things: '*I have a few coins left*' is a more positive expression than '*Few coins remain*'.

Note: You will also find the zero declension (the neuter bit from it) following *etwas* and *nichts* to mean *something [interesting]* or *nothing [good]*. Any adjective is possible, though.

Nominative / Accusative: *etwas Interessantes, nichts Gutes*
Dative: *etwas Altem*
The genitive is rarely used like this, but would be *nichts Neuen*
The first letter of the adjective is always capitalised for this.

Sometimes adjectives are shortened to make them easier to pronounce or so that they sound better. Let's take *teuer* (expensive) as an example. Putting it after the noun causes no problems: *das Buch ist teuer.* However, when it goes before the noun, it loses an 'e': *das ist ein teures Buch.* Other words that act in this way include *dunkel, sauer* and *miserabel,* and then there's *hoch*, which loses its 'c': *ein hoher Berg.*

The final basic point on adjectives is that place names can become adjectives. This is normally just for bigger, better-known cities. All you have to do is add '-er' to the place name, regardless of the following noun's number, case or gender: instead of *der Dom in Berlin* you can just say *der Berliner Dom.* Don't forget that sometimes adjectives shorten, like for Basel in Switzerland: *nach der Basler Fasnacht (– after the Basel Carnival,* with '-er' being the right dative ending here).

Note: Often, people drop marks in their exams because they forget to make adjectives in front of the noun agree, not because they don't know how to make them agree. This is because we don't do it in English. So, think of the Checking Rules for every time you write in German; 'Part 2' on pg. 62 applies to the agreement of adjectives. However, first and foremost, make sure you remember the Golden Rule and don't forget grammar!

Comparison of Adjectives

So, we've seen adjectives in their basic form: 'the dog is big', 'the big dog'. What happens, though, if we want to say 'this dog is *bigger* than that dog' or 'this dog is the *biggest* dog'? Here, 'bigger' is known as the comparative form and 'biggest' the superlative form of the adjective 'big'. In German, conveniently, the same sort of endings are used ('-er' and '-(e)st'). An important difference is that, in English, you say things like 'more favourable', rather than 'favourabler', but in German, you always use endings to indicate the comparative or the superlative forms.

Let's take *nett* as an example. We can say the following:

'Der Mann ist nett. Er ist ein netter Mann. Dieser Mann ist netter als jener. Er ist ein netterer Mann. Dieser Mann ist am nettesten. Er ist der netteste Mann.'

'The man is nice. He is a nice man. This man is nicer than that man. He is a nicer man. This man is the nicest. He is the nicest man.'

With these sentences, note how adjective endings are required when the adjective goes before the noun, marked in yellow. Do not get confused between *netter* before the noun and *netter* afterwards. In the first instance, the '-er' is a normal adjective ending. In the second, the '-er' tells us it's a comparative. Also note how the superlative works after the noun: *am* plus the superlative adjective with an '-en' ending. (Don't be tempted to put a capital letter on the front here, even though it looks a lot like a noun!)

So, we've got the basics. Add '-er' to an adjective in it's simple form to make it a comparative, or '-(e)st' to make it a superlative, plus the correct adjective endings as required.

Complications arise with many single-syllable adjectives that need an umlaut:

Normal	Translation	Comparative	Superlative
dumm	stupid	dümmer	am dümmesten
groß	big, tall	größer	am größten
jung	young	jünger	am jüngsten
kalt	cold	kälter	am kältesten
kurz	short	kürzer	am kürzesten
lang	long	länger	am längsten
schwach	weak	schwächer	am schwächsten
stark	strong	stärker	am stärksten
warm	warm	wärmer	am wärmsten

We've been putting an 'e' in brackets when talking about superlatives ('-(e)st'). As you can see in the table, sometimes there's an 'e', sometimes not. It's just something to learn, but you'll get a feeling of when there should be an 'e' eventually.

Then, of course, is everyone's favourite: the irregulars! You will have been using at least a few of these without realising it, partly because they're similar to their English equivalents. Watch out for the 'c's that come and go for *hoch* and *nah*, as we've already seen.

Normal		Comparative		Superlatives	
gut		besser		am besten	das beste
	good		better	best	the best
hoch		höher		am höchsten	das höchste
	high		higher	highest	the highest
nah		näher		am nächsten	das nächste
	near		nearer	nearest	the nearest
viel		mehr		am meisten	das meiste
	much		more	most	the most
wenig		weniger		am wenigsten	das wenigste
	little	less , fewer		least , fewest	the least

We've now covered how to say things positively: 'more important', 'the most important'. However, what happens for 'less important' or 'the least important'?

The answer: pretty much the same way we do it in English. Use *weniger* plus the normal form of the adjective, if you're not going to use its opposite:

Jetzt ist er weniger glücklich. – He's less / not as happy now.
Jetzt ist er trauriger. – He's sadder now.
Das ist am unwichtigsten. – That's the least important (thing). – Das ist am wenigsten wichtig.

Going all the way back to where we started with the comparison of adjectives, we used *als* to say 'than' in *Dieser Mann ist netter als jener.* Don't worry about dieser and jener; they're not that important, but they can be useful for comparing 'this one' to 'that one'. Basically, they work just like the definite articles, *der, die, das,* etc. You should be able to see, then, that both *dieser* and *jener* are in the nominative. This is because you can say: 'this man is nicer than that one **is**', and *sein,* or 'to be', always goes with the nominative. (See pg. 119.)

Anyway, we use *als* when something / someone is bigger or smaller, stronger or weaker, richer or poorer than something / someone else:

Er ist größer als ich. – He is bigger than me.

However, if the two things / people are just as big, small, rich, etc. as the other, then we use *so...wie*:

Sie ist so groß wie ich. – She is as big as I am.
Er ist genauso reich wie ich. – He is just as rich as I am.

Additionally, you can use noch and viel to qualify the adjective:

Der Film war noch / viel spannender als das Buch. – The film was even / much more exciting than the book.

Adverbs

Adverbs in German are essentially the same as the matching adjective, but without any agreement:

Er ist ein scheller Fahrer. Er fährt schnell. – He is a quick driver. He drives quickly.

In most cases, this works for the comparative and superlative forms too:

Er läuft am langsamsten. – He runs the slowest.

Watch out, again, for the irregulars, including:

Normal		Comparative		Superlatives	
viel		mehr		am meisten	
	much		more		most
bald		früher		am frühsten	
	soon		sooner		soonest
gern		lieber		am liebsten	
	gladly	more gladly		most gladly	

You could use all three forms of *gern* one after another in an oral exam, in order to demonstrate your knowledge of the comparison of adverbs! *lieber* is often translated as 'prefer', and a nicer translation of *am liebsten* is 'most of all':

Ich singe gern, ich sehe lieber fern, aber am liebsten lese ich informative Bücher. – I like singing, I prefer watching television, but I like reading informative books most of all.

There are also some special superlative adverbs, which are good to know:

meistens – mostly

mindestens – at least

schnellstens – as quickly as possible

strengstens – very strictly

Das Rauchen ist strengstens verboten. – Smoking is strictly forbidden.

A couple of grade-boosting phrases that you can use are:

1) immer + comparative adjective / adverb – more and more

Es wird hier immer wärmer. – It's getting hotter and hotter here.

2) je + comparative..., desto + comparative... – the more..., the more...

Je mehr man isst, desto dicker wird man. – The more you eat, the fatter you become.

Tip: Watch out for the word order here:

Je + comparative + subject + verb, desto + comparative + verb + subject.

And remember that comma in the middle!

Nouns

Nouns are a heck of lot more difficult in German than they are in English. All we have to worry about in English is whether a noun is singular or plural. This is called **number**. If there's more than one of something it'll be plural, if its existence is singular, it'll be… singular. Of course, you've already noticed that verbs also have this singular and plural distinction.

Nouns in German, like in other European languages, each have a **gender**. We're kept on our toes by there being three genders to look out for: masculine, feminine and neuter. This means that a German table is masculine (*der Tisch*), German art is feminine (*die Kunst*) and German girls are neuter (*das Mädchen*). This last one is constantly under debate, but strictly-speaking they are linguistically neuter. Find out more from pg. 115 onwards.

The final main aspect of German nouns is that they each have a **case**, depending on how they are used in a sentence. This is the one that lots of people struggle with, because they've never seen it before, unless they happen to be familiar with Latin, Greek or Russian.

We'll be dealing with all of these in this section, so take a deep breath! Also, remember that **all German nouns are capitalised**!

In an Exam

The first thing to note is that if you are given a noun in a reading comprehension or an essay title, do not then use it in an answer or an essay in the wrong gender. This just shows you are careless and gives an examiner completely the wrong impression. There have been many examples of people making this stupid mistake, losing themselves marks. On the whole, you have to trust the paper, as it's checked lots of times before you sit it!

GOLDEN RULE :
DON'T GET NOUN GENDERS WRONG IF YOU ARE GIVEN THEM

GCSE GERMAN | 115

So, aside from that, you need to try and learn the genders of words as part of your vocab learning, but in reality it is not as important as learning the words themselves and can be pretty difficult to remember. So, here is a dummy's guide to working out the gender of a word which will work the vast majority of the time.

The Rules of Sex

There are always exceptions, and we will give you a few of them if they are important for you to know... If they are pretty rare words, we're not going to waste your time saying you should learn them because there are more important things to be concentrating on. So, how do you 'work out' the gender of any given noun?

To start with, over 90% of nouns with two syllables which end in '-e' are feminine (*die Lampe, die Reise*). Over 90% of nouns which start with 'Ge-' are neuter (*das Gesetz, das Gespräch*). 70% of nouns ending in '-nis' are neuter (*das Ereignis, das Bedürfnis*); the rest are feminine (*die Erkenntnis, die Erlaubnis*).

All gerunds (infinitives used as nouns) are neuter too: *das Essen* (*eating, food*), *das Schreiben* (*writing*).

Nouns with the following endings are usually, if not always, masculine:

Ending	Example(s)	Exception(s)
-ant	der Konsonant, der Diamant	
-ast	der Kontrast	
-ich	der Teppich	
-ig	der König	
-ismus	der Kapitalismus, der Sozialismus, der Journalismus	
-ling	der Schmetterling	
-ner	der Rentner	
-or	der Motor	das Labor
-us	der Rhythmus	das Genus

Nouns with the following meanings are generally masculine:

Meaning	Example(s)	Exception(s)
Male humans and animals	der Mann, der Arzt, der Hirsch	
Seasons, months, days of the week	der April, der Montag	
Weather, wind, points of the compass	der Nebel, der Wind, der Regen, der Norden	das Gewitter, das Eis, das Wetter
Makes of car	der Audi, der Mercedes	
Monetary units	der Euro, der Dollar	das Pfund
Alcoholic drinks	der Wein, der Wodka	das Bier
Names of mountains and lakes	der Berg, der See	die Zugspitze

In the table above, you'll see that *der See – lake*. However, it's important to realise that lots of German words out there change their meaning depending on their gender. In this way, *die See – sea*. Also, *die Steuer – tax*, but *das Steuer – steering wheel*!

Nouns with the following endings are usually, if not always, feminine:

Ending	Example(s)	Exception(s)
-a	die Pizza	das Sofa
-anz / -enz	die Eleganz	
-ei	die Bücherei, die Partei	das Ei
-heit / -keit	die Freiheit, die Krankheit	
-ie	die Biologie, die Komödie, die Industrie	
-ik	die Musik	
-in	die Freundin	der Urin, das Benzin
-schaft	die Herrschaft, die Naturwissenschaft, die Freundschaft	
-sion / -tion	Die Explosion	
-tät	die Universität, die Relativität	
-ung	die Lösung, die Bedeutung, die Zeitung	
-ur	die Natur	das Abitur

Nouns with the following meanings are generally feminine:

Meaning	Example(s)	Exception(s)
Female humans and animals	die Frau, die Ärztin, die Ricke	das Mädchen, das Fräulein
Aeroplanes, motorbikes, ships	die Boeing, die Titanic	
Rivers in Germany	die Weser, die Donau	der Rhein
Names of numerals	die Eins, die Drei	

Nouns with the following endings are usually, if not always, neuter:

Ending	Example(s)	Exception(s)
-chen	das Mädchen, das Kaninchen	
-lein	das Buchlein, das Fräulein	
-ma	das Drama	die Firma
-ment	das Appartement	der Zement
-el	das Viertel	der Gürtel
-tum	das Eigentum, das Königtum	der Reichtum
-um	das Album	der Konsum

As we mentioned earlier, just as it's weird for people learning German as a foreign language, many Germans don't like how *'the girl'* in German is *'das Mädchen'* i.e. a neuter noun. Nowadays, lots of people say *das Mädchen* and then refer to her as *sie*, but for the purposes of your exams, stick with *es*, because it's grammatically correct. The same goes for *das Fräulein*. The issue arises because '-chen' and '-lein' are diminutive suffixes, which have always led to a neuter noun.

Nouns with the following meanings are generally neuter:

Meaning	Example(s)	Exception(s)
Young human and animals	das Kind, das Baby	der Junge
Metals, chemicals	das Gold, das Eisen	der Stahl, die Bronze
Letters of the alphabet	das Ypsilon	
Continents, countries towns	das Europa, das Deutschland	die Vereinigten Staaten (m), die Schweiz

Plural Nouns

So, how do you make a noun plural?

In English, it's generally pretty easy and normally involves whacking an '-s' at the end of your selected word. In German, the process isn't quite so obvious, so when you look a word up in the dictionary, it'll tell you how to form the plural.

Formation		Singular Example	Plural Example
no ending	(-)	der Autofahrer das Feuer	die Autofahrer die Feuer
no ending but add an umlaut	(")	der Bruder die Mutter	die Brüder die Mütter
add an -e at the end	(-e)	das Getränk der Verein	die Getränke die Vereine
add an -e at the end and an umlaut	("e)	die Hand der Flug	die Hände die Flüge
add -er at the end and an umlaut if possible	(-er)/("er)	das Kind das Rad	die Kinder die Räder
add either an -n or -en at the end	(-n)/(-en)	die Droge die Mahlzeit	die Drogen die Mahlzeiten
add an -s at the end	(-s)	das Auto das Foto	die Autos die Fotos

What do we mean by 'add an umlaut if possible'? It's possible to add an umlaut if the main, stressed vowel of the word (so not the 'u' of the prefix 'Un-'!) is an 'a', an 'o' or a 'u'. Therefore, you can't add umlauts to 'e's and 'i's or vowels which already have umlauts! Also, most of these 'possible words' are monosyllabic. Take the example above: *der Rad* (*wheel*). Its plural form ends '-er' and you can add an umlaut because it's an 'a'.

When you learn your vocab, you should also be learning not only the gender of each word, but also how to form its plural. If you do this now, you'll notice more patterns and have a feel for which kind of plural is required.

It might be worth knowing, though, that the plural and singular forms of a feminine word are always different. Only two feminine words add just the umlaut: *die Mutter, die Tochter.* There is only one neuter word that does this: *das Kloster.* No feminine words end in '-er' in the plural, and only one neuter word ends in an '-e' and has an umlaut: *das Floß.*

Cases

There are four cases in German: Nominative, Accusative, Genitive and Dative. Cases indicate the role of a noun or a pronoun in a sentence or a 'clause'. Each case is used for a different purpose. A noun can only be in one case at a time and there is always a correct case. Cases matter!

Case	Uses	Example(s)
Nominative	The subject of the sentence goes into the nominative case	**Der Junge** macht seine Hausaufgaben.
	Used with verbs like *sein* – in the example, both *ich* and *ein kleiner Mann* refer to the same person	**Ich** bin **ein kleiner Mann**.
Accusative	The direct object of a transitive verb (see pg. 98) goes into the accusative case	Der Junge macht **seine Hausaufgaben**.
	Used after certain prepositions (often to indicate motion or a change of state)	Ich tue es für **meine Schwester**. Ich fahre in **die Stadt**. (in – into)
	Used to show how long something is / was / will be done	Ich arbeitete **den ganzen Tag**.
	Used in set phrases when you're greeting someone or in standard wishes (e.g. *Congratulations!*)	**Guten Tag! Guten Abend! Gute Nacht!** **Herzlichen Glückwunsch!**
Genitive	Shows possession, or when you might say 'of the' or 'of a' in English (e.g. the speed of the horse)	Das Auto **meines Freunds** ist am schnellsten. Die Geschwindigkeit **eines Pferdes** ist erstaunlich.
	Also used after a small number of prepositions	Trotz **des schlechten Wetters** ging ich aus.

Dative	The indirect object of a transitive verb goes in the dative case	Ich habe **meiner Schwester** ein Geschenk gebracht.
	Some verbs 'take the dative' — their object is in the dative, not the accusative	Ich helfe **meinen Eltern** jeden Tag zu Hause.
	Used to show possession (with parts of body and clothing) - see the relevant Golden Nugget	Ich habe **mir** das Bein gebrochen.
	Used after some prepositions	Sie spielt Tischtennis sehr oft mit **ihrem Freund**.
	Also used with lots of adjectives (with the sense of 'to me', 'to him', etc.)	Das ist **mir** zu teuer! Es ist **mir** kalt. / **Mir** ist kalt.

It is essential that you know the cases, how to form them and what they're for. Any queries you have about prepositions - perhaps you're wondering which prepositions take which case - should be answered on the following page.

Prepositions

With cases fresh in the mind, let's have a look a prepositions - words like: in, on, under, through, along, with, etc. There are a fair few of them... but not too many to learn! Prepositions are words which connect nouns or pronouns (see pg. 125) to other elements of a sentence. You'll see many of them in Time / Manner / Place phrases (see pg. 131). The noun or pronoun which the preposition refers to goes into one of the accusative, genitive or dative cases. It is part of your job to learn which case the preposition goes with... and there are a number of catches!

Most prepositions come before the noun they refer to. Where this isn't the case has been shown.

Prepositions with the accusative

Preposition	Meaning	Example(s)
bis	as far as (a place),	Ich fahre nur bis Berlin.
	until (a time)	Bis 1989 lebte sie in Österreich.
durch	through (a place),	Mein Vater fuhr durch das Dorf.
	by (a thing – used in passive sentences)	Berlin wurde 1961 durch die Mauer geteilt.
für	for / on behalf of	Sieben Wochen lang hat er wenig für uns getan.
gegen	against (something physical)	Sie schwamm gegen den Strom. Gegen die Wand...
ohne	without	Das taten sie ohne mein Wissen.
pro	per, every	Sie läuft dreimal pro Woche. Das kostet 8 Euro pro Person.
um	around, about (a place),	Er geht um den Sportplatz.
	at (a time),	Um fünf Uhr...
	concerning	Im Text geht es um eine Beziehung.
wider	against (feelings or emotions)	Wider seinen Willen...

There are other prepositions which take the accusative, but they're either too rare to mention, or they'll be coming up in a bit...

Prepositions with the dative

Preposition	Meaning	Example(s)
aus	out of (a place)	aus dem Haus
	made out of (a material)	aus Leder
außer	except for, apart from	außer meiner Freundin
bei	at (the house of),	beim Bäcker
	near to,	bei München
	in a set of circumstances,	bei kaltem Wetter
	while, by	beim Tanzen
entgegen	against, contrary to	seinem Befehl entgegen – comes before or after noun
gegenüber	opposite	Ich setzte mich ihm gegenüber – comes <u>after</u> a pronoun, and before or after a noun
laut	according to	Laut Berichten, laut Gesetz, laut Tim
mit	with	mit meiner Schwester zusammen, Was ist mit dir los?
nach	after / past (in time),	zwanzig nach elf / nach der Arbeit
	to (a place),	nach Frankreich
	according to	meiner Meinung nach – comes after noun
seit	since,	seit dem Fall der Berliner Mauer…
	for (a period of time)	Seit zehn Jahren wohne ich hier.
von	(away) from (a place),	Er fuhr von Berlin nach Frankfurt.
	by (a person – used in passive sentences)	Die Kekse wurden von dem Jungen versteckt.
	of (– often replaces a genitive)	ein Vetter von uns
zu	to (a place / person), & lots of other uses	Er ging zu seiner Tante.

Again, there are others, some generally not that useful, others coming up soon.

Prepositions with the genitive

Preposition	Meaning	Example(s)
(an)statt	instead of	Statt eines Briefes schickte sie ihm eine Postkarte.
trotz	despite, in spite of	Trotz des furchtbaren Wetters ging er aus.
während	during	Während des Sommers…
wegen	because of	Wegen des Regens war der Verkehr stark.

Once more, there are indeed other less common ones like these.

Prepositions with the accusative or the dative

Now for the fun stuff. There are a number of prepositions which can go either with the accusative or with the dative, but their meaning changes depending on which one (so it's not a free choice!). As a general rule, if there's movement towards relevant noun or pronoun, it'll be in the accusative, and if there's rest or movement in / at a place, the noun or pronoun will be in the dative. (Also, pay particular attention to the position of *entlang* in relation to the noun.)

Colour coding: Accusative, Dative

Preposition	Meaning	Example(s)
an	at, to, on (a vertical surface)	Wir hängen das Bild an die Wand. Das Bild hängt an der Wand.
auf	at, to, in, on (a horizontal surface)	Ich stelle die Tasse auf den Tisch. Die Tasse steht auf dem Tisch.
entlang	along	Wir gingen den Fluss entlang. Bäume standen entlang der Bahnlinie.
hinter	behind	Wir gingen hinter das Haus. Hinter dem Haus gibt es einen Garten.
in	in	Wir gehen ins Restaurant. Wir sitzen im Kino. (Contractions – see pg. 137.)
neben	next to, (apart from – just with DAT)	Er stellte die Blumen neben den Schrank. Die Blumen standen neben dem Schrank.

über	over, above, (more than – just when +ACC)	Das Bild hängt über dem Kamin. Die Stadt liegt 1200 Meter über dem Meeresspiegel. Sie ist über zwei Meter groß.
unter	under, less than, (amongst – just when +DAT)	Sie sind unter die Brücke geschwommen. Sie schwimmen unter der Brücke. Du bist hier ja unter Freunden.
vor	in front of, (ago – just time phrases in DAT)	Er stand direct vor mir. Die Sache (– case) kommt vor Gericht. Vor zwölf Jahren…
zwischen	between	Ich setzte mich zwischen sie und ihren Mann. Ich saß zwischen ihr und ihrem Mann.

It's important to understand with these that *Ich setze mich* means 'I sit down' (i.e. movement to somewhere) and that *Ich sitze* means 'I sit' or 'I am sitting' (i.e. no movement), as this kind of thing tells you whether to put the noun in the accusative or the dative, as you can hopefully see. The easiest one to consider is *in: Ich gehe ins Restaurant. Dann bin ich im Restaurant.*

In general, prepositions are very useful and you'll see them everywhere, including in the section on reflexive pronouns, which is coming up.

Pronouns

Pronouns are words which stand in the place of nouns or 'noun phrases' (– the noun, its article (if it has one) and any preceding adjective e.g. 'the black cat').

You will need to be comfortable with **personal** pronouns (including **reflexive** pronouns) and **relative** pronouns. (There are other types of pronoun, including **possessive** pronouns (like 'That book is **mine**'), **demonstrative** pronouns (like 'My house and **the one** my sister owns') and **interrogatives** (like '**which**', '**who**' and '**what**' in questions). You are unlikely to want to use these and there's plenty to be getting on with already! However, you can always ask your teacher about them if you so desire!)

Personal

Really basically, in English, instead of saying 'The woman gave the book to the boy', we can say 'She gave it to him'. German has pretty much the same system, but quite often you won't need *zu* for the 'to' bit, as the dative generally has that sense already. You'll recognise the first column from the verb tables, because, as we saw in the noun section, the subject of the verb goes in the nominative.

Nominative	Accusative	Dative
ich	mich	mir
du	dich	dir
er	ihn	ihm
sie	sie	ihr
es	es	ihm
wir	uns	uns
ihr	euch	euch
sie	sie	ihnen
Sie	Sie	Ihnen

Let's take the English example from above, translated into German. Note that the colouring is: Nominative, Accusative, Dative.

Die Frau hat dem Jungen das Buch gegeben.

becomes:

Sie hat es ihm gegeben.

The personal pronoun quite simply replaces the noun (with its article and/or adjective) which it refers to. Otherwise, it points directly to a person (I, you, we, they, etc.) or a thing (it).

Remember to keep the same number, gender and case, and that 'it' in English might well be *er, sie* or *es* in German. (See the relevant Golden Nugget.)

> **Note:** Whilst we're considering *es*… It's worth pointing out that this personal pronoun also has an 'impersonal' sense, as seen in *es gibt* and *es regnet*. Think about it: when we say *it's raining*, what does the 'it' actually refer to?

> All the forms of *es gibt* can be found on pg. 143.

Reflexive

As promised earlier in this book, here is a table of the reflexive pronouns, which are explained on pg. 100.

Essentially, use these with reflexive verbs like *sich rasieren* and *sich waschen*. Reflexive verbs often have the sense of doing something to oneself ('I shave myself', 'I wash myself'), but sometimes they have an accusative object and the *sich* bit goes into the dative. Don't worry, though, because the only changes to the accusative reflexive pronouns are in the *ich* and *du* forms:

Nominative	Accusative	Dative
ich	mich	mir
du	dich	dir
er/sie/es/ singular noun	sich	sich
wir	uns	uns
ihr	euch	euch
sie/ plural noun	sich	sich
Sie	Sich	Sich

Note that the colouring in the examples below is: Nominative, Accusative, Dative. Basically, use the accusative column unless there's another noun or pronoun that has to be included.

Ich rasiere mich. Ich wasche mich. – I shave. I wash.

But:

Ich wasche mir den Arm. – I wash my arm.

Lots of the time, the reflexive is followed by a preposition:

Ich interessiere mich für (+ACC) – I'm interested in…

Note that the preposition controls the case of the following noun. See the section before this one on prepositions (which starts on pg. 121).

Relative

Relative pronouns introduce '**relative clauses**', which are subordinate clauses (so, not the main part of a sentence - see pg. 130) that begin with words like 'who', 'which' or 'whose': *The man with the afro,* **who ate my sandwich,** *turned out to be really funny,* **which was great.** In this example sentence, we see the two broad types of relative pronoun. The 'who' refers directly to the person, whereas the 'which' refers to the idea that the man 'turned out to be really funny'.

	Masculine	Feminine	Neuter	Plural
Nominative	der	die	das	die
Accusative	den	die	das	die
Genitive	dessen	deren	dessen	deren
Dative	dem	der	dem	denen

Oh look! We've given you another table! How this one works: you should look backwards / earlier in the sentence for gender and number; forward / later in the sentence for case. What do we mean by that?

(Note that the colouring is: Nominative, Accusative, Genitive, Dative. And don't worry too much about word order yet… there's a section for that, which starts on pg. 130! However, you should notice that the main clause (underlined here) has the same order as it would if the relative clause weren't there.)

Der Baum, den ich gestern gesehen habe, war äußerst groß. – The tree which I saw yesterday was extremely tall.

The relative pronoun in the sentence we've just seen is *den* and its corresponding noun is *der Baum*. Looking backwards, we're dealing with a masculine singular noun here, so it's the *der, den, dessen, dem* column. We get the case from the pronoun's function in the relative clause - looking forwards. This time, it's the object (the subject being *ich*), so the pronoun goes into the accusative case.

Let's look at another:

Die Ärztin, deren Haus sehr sauber ist, ist zu spät zur Arbeit gekommen. – The (female) doctor, whose house is very clean, was late for work.

Looking backwards, the relative pronoun must be singular and female to agree with *die Ärztin*. The subject of the relative clause is *Haus*, so we're left with the accusative, the dative or the genitive for the case of the pronoun. It's just about what makes sense. It can't be something like 'The doctor, which house is very clean' - only 'whose' fits here.

Ich habe jetzt den Artikel gelesen, der meiner Mutter gefallen hatte. – I have now read the article which had pleased my mum / which my mum had liked.

For this one, it's a little bit different, because the relative pronoun goes with *den Artikel*, which is the object of the main clause. Don't be tempted to make the pronoun accusative too: we only look back for gender and number (masculine, singular). The *Artikel* is the subject of the relative clause, so it must be nominative (*der*).

> **Note:** If you don't know or have forgotten why *meiner Mutter* is dative... Remember that the expression is *das gefällt mir* ('it's pleasing to me' – I like it). What's above is just the phrase in the pluperfect tense. (See pg. 95 for info on this particular tense.)

Next up is prepositions in relative clauses! For this, consider older people or people who like to show off a bit with grammar. They might insist upon a rule that prepositions do not end sentences in English. (*This is something **with** which we are familiar.*) Think about this, as it's how it works in German: the preposition goes in front of the relative pronoun, and then the pronoun changes its case depending on which preposition you use. See pg. 121 for rules on this kind of thing.

Sie sind die Mädchen, mit denen *ich gern Tischtennis spiele.* – They are the girls with whom I like to play table tennis.

Now, be careful: *die Mädchen* is plural. If we had forgotten that it's *das Mädchen*, as it looks like it could be a singular noun here, the *sind* tells us it must be plural, so we're looking at the last column in the table. *mit* takes the dative, so the relative pronoun must be *denen*. (And yes, we put 'whom'. It just sounds more grown-up.)

The final type you have to contend with is when the relative pronoun refers the the whole idea. Basically, you use *was* for this, although things become rather more complicated when you add in prepositions. Not at all needed to get a high grade, though, but ask your teacher if you're curious.

Unsere Großeltern konnten unser Fußballspiel *sehen,* **was** *wir toll gefunden haben.* – Our grandparents were able to see our football match, which we found great.

What 'we' found great was not 'our football match', but the fact that 'our grandparents were able to see it'. Otherwise, the relative pronoun would have been *das* (accusative, neuter, singular).

Possessive Adjectives

There's not much to be said about these that hasn't already been made clear, but here is a list of possessive adjectives and the pronouns they go with.

Pronoun	Possessive	Meaning
ich	**mein**	my
du	**dein**	your
er	**sein**	his , its
sie	**ihr**	her , its
es	**sein**	its
wir	**unser**	our
ihr	**euer**	your
sie	**ihr**	your (polite form)
Sie	**Ihr**	their

To see how these decline (i.e. change to match the noun), go to pg. 107. You will need to replace 'ein-' with 'mein-' or 'unser-', etc., but the endings are as in the indefinite table. See also the Golden Nugget about ihr, Ihr and ihr on pg. 141.

The Art of Commas and Word Order

Whilst it may seem ridiculous that we've dedicated a section of this book to commas and word order, there are good reasons for this apparent madness. Commas in German are actually quite important. They split up clauses, and split up verbs, and are not placed willy-nilly, in contrast to how most people use them in English. Now think about word order in English. 'Today have I the most beautiful girl in the world seen, with whom I for ever to dance want.' Yes, you can probably get the gist of this bizarre 'sentence', but it doesn't exactly make sense. It's written how the German translation would be written. German has its own logic as far as word order is concerned.

Sentence structure – different clauses

There are three types of clause in German. The difference between them is the position of the main or 'finite' verb.

Type of clause	Example
Main clause statements In a main clause statement, the finite verb comes in the second position. This means that there can be one and only <u>one element</u> before it, like its <u>subject</u>, <u>one of TMP</u> (see the next page) or a <u>subordinate clause</u>.	<u>Markus</u> **fährt** heute nach Hause. <u>Heute</u> **fährt** Markus nach Hause. <u>Nachdem er London besucht hatte</u>, **ist** Markus nach Hause gefahren.
Subordinate clause In a subordinate clause, such as a relative clause or a *dass* clause, the finite verb comes last. This can mean that the verb and its subject are split up by some distance.	Markus, der heute nach Hause **fährt**, ist müde. Ich weiß, dass Markus heute nach Hause **fährt**.
Questions and commands In both questions and commands, the finite verb comes first, followed by its <u>subject</u> (if applicable). However, any question word like *was* or *wohin* comes before the finite verb.	**Fährt** <u>Markus</u> heute nach Hause? Wohin **fährt** Markus heute? **Fahren** <u>Sie</u> heute nach Hause! (If you address Markus as *Sie*) **Fahr** heute nach Hause! (If you address Markus as *du*)

Treat your sentences with a little TMP

You may well have heard people talking about 'Time, **M**anner, **P**lace' in connection with word order. You should understand this as the way a basic sentence is constructed. Note that the colouring for this is: Time, Manner, Place.

Ich fahre um drei Uhr mit dem Auto in die Stadt.

Time	Fairly self-explanitory, but also includes *am Sonnstag*, phrases with *seit, später, nachmittags* (*in the afternoon*), *nie, schon, sofort* (*immediately*)…
Manner	Generally how something was / is / will be done: *mit dem Zug, gern, vielleicht, natürlich, nicht, langsam, gut, leider, hoffentlich, wahrscheinlich* (*probably*)…
Place	Not difficult to deduce, but remember: *hier, da, dort, in der Nähe, draußen* (*outside*), *drinnen* (*inside*), *zu Hause, bei mir, in meinem Zimmer, in Deutschland*…

A brief word on commas

Look at the full-sentence examples we give you and try to understand why a comma has been put where it is. Commas separate clauses and verbs, but there are also things like nouns in apposition (where more information is given about a noun afterwards and without a verb).

Ich spiele gern Fußball, aber ich spiele lieber Tennis.
Nachdem wir ins Restaurant gegangen waren, haben wir viel Essen bestellt.
Wenn ich älter bin, werde ich Lehrbücher schreiben.
Ich mag ihn wegen seiner Persönlichkeit, und weil er gut aussehend ist!
Als ich jünger war, sah ich viele Filme.
Der Mann, ein ausgebildeter Arzt, wohnt in Konstanz, einer großen Stadt.

Note the cases used in this last one. *Der Mann* and *ein Arzt* are both nominative (both the subject), and *Konstanz* and *einer Stadt* are both dative (to go with the preposition *in*).

What do I do with…? – An aid for sentence construction

Note: If you're looking for help with separable verbs, turn to pg. 101, where there is a comprehensive guide. They are, of course, quite heavily linked to word order and sentence structure.

Phrases

Now we're going to deal with where verbs go in certain cicumstances. Normally this will involve sending something to the end of the clause, inverting the verb and its subject or sticking with the subject-verb-object order.

We've picked out just the highlights of the phrases you'll find in Section II of this book. Try to recognise the patterns involved. Look at pg. 50 for more examples.

Type	Word order	Example
weil, da, obwohl	<u>finite verb</u> goes to end	Obwohl ich nicht genug Geld <u>hatte</u>, habe ich das Spiel toll gefunden, weil ich viel gegessen <u>habe</u>.
um…zu, ohne…zu	<u>infinitive</u> goes to end (after zu)	Ich arbeite, um Geld zu verdienen.
dass	<u>finite verb</u> goes to end	Ich finde, dass sie hübsch ist.
denn, und, aber	normal verb order	…aber ich mag den Film nicht.
nachdem, bevor	<u>finite verb</u> goes to end	Nachdem ich Cola getrunken <u>hatte</u>, fühlte ich mich sehr glücklich.
später, dannach, außerdem	invert <u>finite verb</u>	Außerdem <u>habe</u> ich meine Hausaufgaben gemacht.

Notice how, as we've already said, the **finite verb** in the main clause will invert following a subordinate clause:

*Nachdem ich Cola getrunken hatte, **fühlte** ich <u>mich</u> sehr glücklich.*

Also, have a look at where the <u>pronoun</u> has gone. *mich* is as early in the clause as it can be, which will be the same for most pronouns.

Compound tenses

Past – In the next several examples, *viel* is just standing in for whatever you might have in the middle of your sentence. Notice how the **past participle** is at the end, unless the phrase sends the <u>finite verb</u> to the end. With the final clause, just the main infinitive goes after the *zu*.

Ich <u>habe</u> viel **gearbeitet**.
Außerdem <u>habe</u> ich viel **gearbeitet**.
Bevor ich viel **gearbeitet** <u>hatte</u>,…
Ohne viel **gearbeitet** zu haben,… (– without having worked a lot…)

Future – This will be the same if you're using subjunctive II of werden (würden) plus an infinitive (see pg. 94). Notice how the **infinitive** is at the end, unless the phrase sends the <u>finite verb</u> to the end.

Ich <u>werde</u> viel **arbeiten**.
Später <u>werde</u> ich viel **arbeiten**.
Obwohl ich viel **arbeiten** <u>werde</u>,…

Modals

Modals come with infinitives. This is where things can get much more complicated, but it's still not impossible to understand! Notice how:

the modal sends the infinitive to the end,
werden sends the infinitive to the end and
hätten (subjunctive II of haben) sends the past participle of *müssen* (which is, conveniently, the infinitive) to the end

Tense	English	German
Present	I must work a lot.	Ich muss viel arbeiten.
Simple Past	I had to work a lot.	Ich musste viel arbeiten.
'Conditional'	I would have to work a lot.	Ich müsste viel arbeiten.
Future	I will have to work a lot.	Ich werde viel arbeiten müssen.
'Conditional Perfect'	I would have had to work a lot.	Ich hätte viel arbeiten müssen.

Note: The 'conditional' and the 'conditional perfect' aren't really tenses in German. See pg. 93 for info about subjunctive II.

For the top three (present, simple past, 'conditional'), things work as expected when we include a *dass* or a *weil / obwohl*... The <u>finite verb</u> (the modal) goes to the end of the subordinate clause:

Obwohl ich viel arbeiten <u>muss</u>,
finde ich Zeit, mit meinen Freunden zu sprechen.
Obwohl ich viel arbeiten <u>musste</u>,
fand ich Zeit, mit meinen Freunden zu sprechen.
Obwohl ich viel arbeiten <u>müsste</u>,
würde ich Zeit finden, mit meinen Freunden zu sprechen.

.. but with the last two (future, 'conditional perfect'), things are a bit different, because of the **double-infinitive rule**. We said earlier that a model's (normal) past participle is the same as its infinitive. Well, someone along the line of the development of the German language someone saw two infinitives together and understood this as a brick wall. So, what the rule states is that the <u>finite verb</u> (which would normally go at the end in a *weil / obwohl* clause or in a *dass* clause) can't get past the **double-infinitive**:

Obwohl ich viel <u>werde</u> **arbeiten müssen**,
werde ich Zeit finden, mit meinen Freunden zu sprechen.
Obwohl ich viel <u>hätte</u> **arbeiten müssen**,
hätte ich Zeit gefunden, mit meinen Freunden zu sprechen.

It looks so wrong, but it is so right.

There's not a lot in the German language which is weirder than that, so if you're coping, brilliant! If you're not, seriously don't worry - a good grade is still very possible! Anyway, don't use that more than once in your essay, because you will just be wasting words - and there aren't many Germans who would say such a thing in everyday conversation, so think twice before using the construction in your oral...

Of course, if you do manage to use it, you can always change the modal from *müssen* to one that is more suitable for your sentence!

The double-infinitive construction looks even more impressive when it is used in a *wenn* sentence.

Remember how these work?

German	English
Wenn ich 17 Jahre alt bin, werde ich fahren können.	When I'm 17, I will be able to drive.
Wenn ich 17 Jahre alt wäre, würde ich fahren können.	If I were 17, I would be able to drive.
Wenn ich 17 Jahre alt gewesen wäre, hätte ich fahren können.	If I had been 17, I would have been able to drive.

The ones with the subjunctive (the second and third types of *wenn* sentence) must balance: both sides of the comma are the same formation. Just use a normal subjunctive II for the second type, and then, for the third, the suitable auxiliary verb in subjunctive II (*hätte / wäre* – see pg. 98 for which to use) and a past participle. It's only more complex because modals take an infinitive.

> **Tip:** Previously, we have said that *ich könnte* is used instead of *ich würde können*. This is generally true, but in a *wenn* sentence where you are trying to get across the sense of *I would be able to* as opposed to simply *I could*, it may be better to use *ich würde können*. However, either will get you your marks here as they are both subjunctive II! Just remember that you should never say *ich würde haben* or *ich würde sein*... These always become *ich hätte* and *ich wäre* respectively.

So, you adapt the last type of *wenn* sentence and include a double-infinitive...

Wenn ich <u>hätte</u> fahren können, wäre ich der glücklichste Mensch auf der Welt gewesen.	If I had been able to drive, I would have been the happiest man in the world.

Again, these bits of grammar are pretty advanced, which does mean that they will impress an examiner, **but only if you get them right**. So, only consider using things like a complex *wenn* sentence with a 'conditional perfect' and a double-infinitive construction once you are confident about the more fundamental aspects of German grammar!

Tips and Tricks – Golden Nuggets to Remember

Nugget	Examples
Ferien The word *Ferien* (holidays) is never singular. It's used when you're talking about the school holidays and not really a specific trip somewhere. (You would use *der Urlaub* for that.)	Wo fahrt ihr in den **Ferien** hin? – Where are you going in the holidays? (though the sense is: 'Where are you going on holiday?') Heute plane ich für die **Ferien**. – Today I'm planning for the holidays.
Viel / Viele This is simple, but people often forget: *viel* is followed by a singular noun, *viele* is followed by a plural noun. In other words, when you would say 'much' in English, use *viel* and when you would say 'many' in English, use *viele*. *Viel* is also used as an adverb. If you're doing something 'a lot'.	Ich habe zu **viel** gegessen. / Ich habe zu **viel** Essen gegessen. / Ich habe zu **viele** Kekse (biscuits) gegessen. Es gibt immer **viel** zu tun. – There is always much / a lot to do. Wir haben **viel** gelacht. – We laughed a lot.
Home In English, we say 'to go home' and 'to be (at) home'. In German, if you're not home, but are talking about heading towards home, you say *nach Hause*. If you're talking about being at home, it's *zu Hause*. You may be wondering why there's an 'e' at the end of *Haus*. This is just a stylistic thing from older German. Like the 'n' at the end of nouns in the dative plural (e.g. *auf den Tischen*), there used to be an 'e' for dative singular nouns.	Nein, ich mag Partys nicht. Ich bleibe **zu** Hause. Schule ist so langweilig. Ich fahre **nach** Hause. On the Reichstag building it says: DEM DEUTSCHEN VOLKE which means '(dedicated) to the German people'.

Contractions

Lots of prepositions can merge with the definite article.

an + das = ans, an + dem = am
auf + das = aufs
bei + dem = beim
in + das = ins, in + dem = im
um + das = ums
von + dem = vom
zu + dem = zum
zu + der = zur

You do not use contractions with a relative pronoun

Der Park, **in dem** ich sitze, ist groß.

Bei

To say 'at my house', you can also just use *bei*. This works with other nouns too.

bei mir – at mine

bei einem Freund – at a friend's

Countries

When you say **to** a country you almost always use **nach**. The exceptions on the right use **in** with the accusative.

When you want to say in a country, use **in** (with the dative).

As you will have seen in the nouns section, most countries are neuter, but there are some exceptions: e.g. *Switzerland – die Schweiz*

In most cases it's not obvious that normal countries are neuter, because there is no article to be seen.

<u>Normal:</u>

Ich fahre heute nach **Frankreich**.
Ich habe vor, nach **Spanien** zu fliegen.

Als ich in **Deutschland** war, aß ich viele Würste.

<u>Exceptions:</u>

Später werde ich in **die Schweiz** fahren. (in + Acc) Dann werde ich in **der Schweiz** sein. (in + Dat)

Ich will in **die Vereinigten Staaten** fliegen. Ich bin noch nicht in **den Vereinigten Staaten** gewesen.

Nouns are capitalised

As in English, the beginnings of sentences are capitalised, as are proper nouns (names, places). But the Germans don't stop there. All nouns in German are capitalised, but other words (adjectives, adverbs, etc.), even in titles of books and films, are not.

Brauchen wir eigentlich einen Satz hier?

Ich mag **N**ew **Y**ork.

‚**V**on morgens bis mitternachts' ist ein expressionistisches **B**ühnenstück von **G**eorg **K**aiser.

You – the *du* / *Sie* dilemma

In English, there is quite simply one word for 'you'. It's both singular and plural, and can be said to anyone. In other European languages, there's generally more than one word to distinguish between the singular and the plural 'you'. Usually, as in German, there's a polite form and a familiar form, and there can be embarrassment for both parties if *du* and *Sie* are used inappropriately.

However, it's important to note that there are no real rules here. Whether you can call someone *du* or *Sie* isn't always about whether you call them by their first name or not. Social norms change from place to place, even in Germany! Chances are, though, you should address your boss with *Sie* (at least until he / she starts calling you *du*), and, for most, parents will be fine with *du*.

Moods: the imperative

We've discussed the subjunctive mood for a good while (see pg. 93), and talked about the indicative (which is just your normal 'setting'), but there's also the imperative mood, which is used for commands.

There isn't really a time in (I)GCSE when you have to use it, but it may help to recognise it.

Kommen Sie herein! – Come in! (Sie)

Komm herein! – Come in! (du)

Schreib schneller! – Write faster!

Gehen wir! – Let's go!

It

As you've hopefully noticed, German nouns have a gender: masculine, feminine or neuter. After you mention something you might want to refer to it as 'it' rather than repeat the word.

Don't be tempted to use *es* for everything an English speaker might call 'it'. In German, you must use the correct gender of pronoun for the noun (and put it in the right case, of course!).

-Warum ist **die Frau** traurig?

-**Sie** ist traurig wegen des schlechten Wetters.

-Wo ist **mein Hund**?

-Ich habe **ihn** nicht gesehen.

Do not confuse:

sprechen – to speak

sagen – to say

Wo vs. Wohin

Both of these mean 'where?', but they have different sense. *Wo* is used when you're after someone's present location. *Wohin* is for finding out someone's destination. In this way, *wohin* is more 'where to?' than just 'where?'.

Wo bist du?

Wohin fahren Sie?

Wer

This word is forever catching people out. Despite its appearance, *wer* does not mean 'where?' - It means 'who?'!

Wer ist er? Ich habe ihn noch nicht kennengelernt.

Etwas Interessantes

To say *something* + *adjective* in German, you cannot simply say *etwas* + *adjective*, you must capitalise the adjective and add the right ending (depending on the required case - see the neuter singular column in the zero declension table on pg. 108).

You can also say *nothing* + *adjective* by switching *etwas* for *nichts*.

The same goes for *everything* + *adjective*, by using *alles.*

Gesten habe ich **etwas Wichtiges** gesehen. **NOT** etwas wichtig

Ich hoffe, dass **nichts Schlechtes** passieren wird. **NOT** nichts schlecht

„**Alles**, ob **Gutes** oder **Schlechtes**, passiert aus einem Grund." – "Everything, good or bad, happens for a reason."

Jemand Interessantes

As with 'something' and 'nothing' above, you can say 'someone interesting' or 'nobody important' using *jemand* and *niemand*, followed by an adjective with the ending '-es' in the nominative, '-en' in the accusative and '-em' in the dative.

Note that, on their own, *jemand* and *niemand* often have endings (although people are lazy and are increasingly leaving them off), but with the adjective added afterwards, they don't tend to have those endings.

Ich habe **jemand Sonderbaren** kennengelernt.

Sie hat **niemand Wichtigen** gesehen.

Wir haben **jemanden** gesehen.

Es gab **niemanden** im Haus.

Sport treiben

In English you can say 'do sport' or 'play sport', but in German, you can't really say *Sport spielen* - say *Sport treiben*.

Ich **treibe** jeden Tag **Sport**, weil es so wichtig ist, gesund zu bleiben.

NOT ich spiele Sport

Transport

With lots of forms of transport, it's really easing to describe how you're travelling. Looking at it literally, you don't say 'I'm going <u>by</u> car' in German, you say 'I'm going **with the** car'

Ich fahre **mit dem** Bus / Auto / Schiff / Rad / Zug / Flugzeug… (if masculine or neuter noun)

Ich fahre **mit der** U-Bahn / Straßenbahn… (if feminine noun)

Negating sentence

In German, you have to be careful where you put *nicht* in the sentence, as this changes the meaning. In English, the same effect is achieved by intonation - putting a stress on (a) certain word(s).

Wir haben am Mittwoch **nicht** gespielt.

(We didn't play on Wednesday.)

Wir haben **nicht** am Mittwoch gespielt…

(We didn't play on *Wednesday*, [but we did on Saturday].)

Other negatives

noch nicht – not yet

überhaupt nicht – not at all

(broadly speaking) *nicht ein – kein*

Ich habe das **noch nicht** gemacht.

Ich mag Paris **überhaupt nicht**.

Du bist **kein** guter Freund!

Doch

In English, if someone says 'You're not going to the party, are you?' and you say 'Yes', are you going or aren't you?!

In German, you say *nein* to agree to a negative statement and *doch* to disagree with it.

-Ihr geht nicht auf die Party, oder?

-Nein, ich muss meine häuslichen Pflichten erledigen.

-**Doch!** Ich muss einfach da sein!

Date & Time

When you write the date in German, you put *am* then the number of the day followed by a full-stop and then the month, as in the example. If you include the day, it's slightly different.

Writing the time in German is actually very easy. Just use the 24-hour clock and write in as in the example.

Something to be careful about, though. When English speakers say 'half ten', they mean 'half **past** ten' or '10:30'. When German speakers say 'halb zehn', they mean 'half **to** ten' or '09:30'!

Die Vorstellung beginnt **am 7. März** um 16.20 Uhr.

Am Mittwoch, dem 23. Juni, wurde er geboren.

Ich bin **um 18.00 Uhr** angekommen.

Singular subject, singular verb

Lost of students are tempted to put rubbish like *die Familie <u>sind</u>* into their essays on the grounds that a family is made up of multiple people. However, in German, the rules are clear.

Die Familie ist nicht zu Hause.

Familien sind immer bereit.

Sie, Sie and *sie* –

ihr, Ihr and *ihr*

Although you can sometimes work it out by looking at the verb, it's often hard to tell these apart, until you look at the context. *Sie* is not the same as *sie* or *sie* (look at the examples!). If you are not concentrating, you may see *Sie* at the start of a sentence (where it would be capitalised anyway) and get the wrong one!

The same goes for *Ihr* and *ihr* and *ihr*.

'*Sie* + singular verb' will always be 'she' (or 'it' if *sie* refers to a 'thing' which is a feminine noun).

Sie ist ein nettes Mädchen. – She is a nice girl.

Sie sind nett. – You (polite) / They are nice.

Ich denke, dass **sie** nett sind. – I think that they are nice.

Ich denke, dass **Sie** nett sind. – I think that you (polite) are nice.

Ich mag **ihr** Auto. – I like her / their car.

Ich mag **Ihr** Auto. – I like your car. (When speaking to someone you would address as *Sie*.)

Parts of the body / Injuries

Like in other European languages, it's better to use the definite article and a dative pronoun (see pg. 125 onwards) than something like *mein* or *sein* for parts of the body.

Ich habe **mir das Bein** gebrochen.

Ich habe **mir den Fuß** verstaucht. (– I sprained my ankle)

If you cut your finger, there's a special phrase, which uses an accusative pronoun. The finger is still *den Finger*, and not *meinen Finger*, though.

Ich habe **mich** in **den Finger** geschnitten.

Seit + present

In English, we say **I have been doing** something for [5] years. Therefore, students often translate this using *seit* and the perfect tense... However, in German, you need to use the present instead of the perfect.

Ich **klettere seit** zehn Jahren. – I have been climbing for ten years.

Ich **habe seit** mehreren Tagen Fieber. – I've had a fever for several days.

Remember to add the dative plural '-n' to the noun if you've been doing that something for more than one day / month / year (see the examples.)

Pronouncing *ich*

In the oral section of your exam, you'll want your accent to be as authentic as possible. One of the ways students sound like non-native speakers is by mispronouncing *ich*... and you'll say the word a lot!

It should not be 'ick' nor should it be 'isch', but there should be a soft, breathy sound to it. Ask your teacher to say it for you if you are unsure about this. You'll be speaking like a German in no time.

Lots of *es gibt*

In German, *es gibt* means *there is* or *there are*. **It does not change in the plural.** There are lots of different forms of *es gibt* which can be used in your essays to show off your knowledge of tenses.

es gibt – there is / are

es gab – there was / were

es hat... gegeben – there has / have been

es hatte... gegeben – there had been

es wird... geben – there will be

es gäbe – there would be

es wird... gegeben haben – there will have been

es hätte... gegeben – there would have been

es muss... geben – there must be

es hätte... geben müssen – there ought to have been

es sollte... geben – there should be

es hätte... geben sollen – there should have been

es könnte... geben – there could be

es hätte... geben können – there could have been

Note: See pp. 86, 87 and 92 for info on when to use the simple past and when to use the perfect.

The Golden Rules

WRITING EXAM

1. Write what you know, don't write what you don't know
2. Don't write too much - there is a word limit for a reason
3. Use phrases but don't force them - if a sentence sounds unnatural, you will lose marks

ORAL EXAM

4. Say what you know, don't say what you don't know
5. Be prepared but sound spontaneous - use what you have learnt while sounding chatty
6. Expand your answers - give as much detail as possible with reasons and opinions included
7. Breathe slowly and remember: everyone is nervous before their oral!

CONTROLLED ASSESSMENTS

8. Do not use a dictionary in the exam to look up words which were not included in your prepared essay

READING & LISTENING EXAMS

9. You will not understand every word, but you don't need to
10. Know how to manipulate information in the text
11. Answer the question in the right language and tense
12. Give the information you are asked to give

VOCABULARY

13. Learn it in small chunks, but regularly
14. Come up with ways of remembering words
15. Revise vocab

GRAMMAR

16. Don't forget grammar
17. Learn *haben*, *sein* and *werden*
18. Don't get noun genders wrong if you are given them

Your Notes

Books in this Series

Follow Us Online

Discover loads of useful resources and find out about all of our current and future products by joining the Exam Grade Booster community online.

Visit us: www.examgradebooster.co.uk

Follow us: @ExamGradeBoost

Watch us: Exam Grade Booster

Like us: Exam Grade Booster

+1 us: Exam Grade Booster

Write For Us

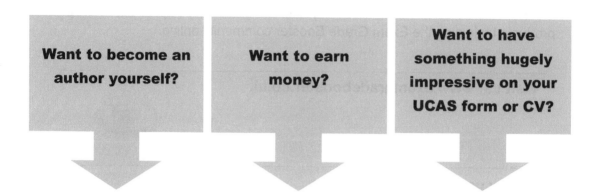

| Want to become an author yourself? | Want to earn money? | Want to have something hugely impressive on your UCAS form or CV? |

Go to **www.examgradebooster.co.uk** and find the **Write for Us** page. This page should have all the information you are after, but if you have any other questions you can contact us via the website. In order to write for us, you will have to complete a very straight-forward application process (there is a short form to fill out at the bottom of the *Write for Us* page). Should you be deemed suitable to write a book, you will be given access to all of our manuscripts, formatting, cover design and branding as well as having the immediate advantage of working with people, just like yourself, who have succeeded in writing their very own books.

Do it:

- Alone
  ... It is possible; Liam wrote *Exam Grade Booster: GCSE French* while he was still at school!
- With your friends
  ... We have a number of books being written by groups of friends to lighten the work load.

Exam Grade Booster

Lightning Source UK Ltd.
Milton Keynes UK
UKOW07f0712310316

271230UK00006B/39/P